Front Porch Parables

Summer 2024

3-Month Seasonal Daily Devotional
June ~ July ~ August

Jeanne Chaffin

Unless otherwise indicated, scripture quotations are taken from the Thompson Chain-Reference, fifth edition Bible, King James Version (KJV), copyright 1988 by B. B. Kirkbride Bible Company.

Scripture quotations marked (TPT) are from The Passion Translation Bible, Passion & Fire Ministries Inc., 2020; (NLT) are from the New Living Translation Bible, Tyndale House Publishers, Inc. 1996; (NKJV) are from New King James Bible, copyright 1982 by Thomas Nelson, Inc.; (NIV) are from the New International Version, copyright 1973, 1978, 1984, 2011 by Biblica, Inc.
All used by permission.

Cover photo taken by author (see June 22 parable)
All interior photos taken by author
Interior watercolor images purchased from artists on Etsy.com
and July sunflower image was downloaded from Pixabay.com
Cover & interior layout design, and book editing by Kathy Mayo (data-junction.com)

ISBN: 9798882178276

Fourth book in the 4-book Seasonal series (all available on Amazon.com)
Follow Jeanne on Facebook for her daily parable posts: facebook.com/jeanne.chaffin

First edition: April 2024
Updated: September 2024

Publisher: Jeanne Chaffin

Printed in the United States of America

About Author

Jeanne Chaffin is a Jesus-follower who passionately loves to study and teach God's Word. She is a farmer's daughter and farmwife, thankful to be living life in the country.

Since her retirement from Central Michigan University as an instructor in Early Childhood Development, she has more opportunities to play with grandchildren and to enjoy life from her front porch. Jeanne is also a former Head Start Teacher and Education Coordinator. She is a founding member of Amazing Grace Church in Breckenridge where she is an active elder, an occasional speaker, and member of the prayer team.

Jeanne has two wonderful sons. Her son Ben followed in his father's footsteps and he and his wife Alyssa farm the family farm. Her son Josh and his wife Wendi work with BigLife Ministries focusing on discipleship and multiplying movements. The family has grown, and now Jeanne is a joyful grandmother of five amazing grandchildren, her favorite role yet!

Mark, Jeanne's high-school sweetheart turned husband of 44 years, now resides in heaven in the presence of the King of Kings. His leaving here was unexpected, but his destination was sure. His love and faith live on through Jeanne, her sons, daughters, grandchildren, and all whose lives he touched and have yet to upgrade their address to a heavenly one.

This book is dedicated to Mark, as he was a master teacher by example and used words when necessary.

Other 3-Month Daily Devotionals by Jeanne Chaffin

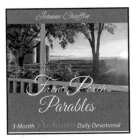

Autumn

Winter

Spring

Introduction

One early morning in June 2021, I was sitting on my front porch reading my Bible while enjoying a cup of hot tea as part of my typical daily Bible study and prayer routine. On that day, I noticed a particularly beautiful sky, snapped a picture, and had the urge to post it on Facebook with the following thought: "6:03 AM beautiful sunrise on the farm. This is the day the Lord has made, I will rejoice and be glad in it (Psalm 118:24). Prayer time."

At that time, the world was still dealing with the Covid-19 pandemic, and I had occasionally posted encouraging Biblical thoughts to Facebook friends, but I hadn't attached a photo to them, nor had the posts been regular. The following morning, I again took a picture and had a strong urge to write a little bit about it and then post it.I continued this day after day. The posts became longer and grew into something more like a teaching, often in the form of an analogy which in Bible times was called a parable.

For someone who has had an aversion to writing throughout their educational career, it was quite a surprise that I was being led to write. I am an avid reader, and my favorite teacher in high school demanded that I learn the art of public speaking. But there were never accolades for my writing abilities in high school, college at Michigan State University, or while gaining my master's degree at Central Michigan University. Writing wasn't my thing. But as posts continued daily, friends began to urge me to publish. I dismissed their crazy notion for quite some time.

Finally, I listened but had no idea how to proceed. The Lord faithfully provided the help I needed when a mutual friend introduced me to Kathy Mayo. Kathy has turned my Facebook posts into the book you hold in your hands. What a talented person she is and what a wonderful friend she has become.

So now you know the beginning of the story. I hope you enjoy my daily devotionals—Front Porch Parables: Autumn published June 2023; Winter published November 2023/ updated September 2024; Spring published January 2024; Summer published January 2024/ updated September 2024.

May the Lord richly bless you.

~Jeanne Chaffin

Oh God, thou art My God;
early will I seek thee:
My soul thirsteth for thee..."
Psalm 63:1a

June
2024

June

~ 1 ~

*T*he colors of the sunrise were beautiful this morning. It amazes me how different the same landscape can appear each morning due to the changes in the clouds and sun. Our lives are filled with variety. No two sunrises are the same and no two people are exactly the same, even if they are identical twins. Personalities and fingerprints are unique.

This morning, I'm surrounded by different bird species with their various pitches of unique bird calls, and a large variety of flowers and trees. Our Father God is creative. When He created, He created with species in mind. If I had been in charge, there would have been one kind of dog; not big Great Danes, little Chihuahuas, and all others in between. Thankfully, I wasn't in charge or we would have a drab and very predictable world. Instead, we see His creative genius everywhere we look.

When I face a dilemma, I tend to give God suggestions on how He could solve the issue—as if He needs my advice. He who spoke the world into existence, who knows the end from the beginning, and created manifold diversification most likely has several solutions much better than I could ever dream of.

For my thoughts are not your thoughts, neither are your ways my ways, saith the LORD. For as the heavens are higher than the earth, so are my ways higher than your ways, and my thoughts than your thoughts.
Isaiah 55:8-9

Instead of trying to assist the Lord with my suggestions regarding what He could do to solve my or the world's problems, I need to bring the issue to Him in prayer, find scripture promises that relate to building my faith, and rest knowing that He is at work. Throughout the day, instead of thinking of ways He could bring things to pass, I need to praise Him, knowing He will take care of it in His way at the right time, better than I could imagine.

(Original post June 2022)

June
~ 2 ~

*I*t's a bit cool on the porch this morning, so I retreated to my recliner and now have the cat on my lap. Sometimes, returning to a shelter is the best decision.

The name of the LORD is a strong tower: The righteous runneth into it, and is safe.
Proverbs 18:10

It intrigues me that His name is a strong tower, and we can run into it. Get that? We can run into His name. It paints a picture in my mind of a mighty fortified castle that lowers its drawbridge, allowing us to run into its safety. But how do we run into His name? In John 16, we're told to pray prayers of petition in Jesus' name.

The Gospel of Mark links the use of the name of Jesus to signs and wonders:

And these miracle signs will accompany those who believe: They will drive out
demons in the power of my name. They will speak in tongues. They will
be supernaturally protected from snakes and from drinking anything
poisonous. And they will lay hands on the sick and heal them.
Mark 16:17-18 TPT

We're to run into His name by using His name in prayer—praying for others and in dangerous situations. It's a powerful name. We can run into it and be safe.

(Original post June 2022)

June
~ 3 ~

*M*y friend and I often walk together in the morning and, of late, have enjoyed the flowers we see along the way. This iris is my recent favorite as its royal purple and bright white beckon attention.

The Lord's artistry and creativity are amazing as He created flowers for differing environments, ranging from cactus blooms in the desert to the iris and other menagerie of flowers we enjoy in the north. He created each to have a specific identifying design. And so were we.

Each of us was created with our own personalized DNA and our own personalized purpose. None of us were a mistake—a surprise maybe—but we were no blunder. And each of us brings our own special set of gifts and abilities to this world.

The Lord beckons us all to a relationship with him. In Him, we find purpose and fulfill destiny.

He has done this so that every person would long for God, feel their way to him, and find him—for he is the God who is easy to discover! It is through him that we live and function and have our identity...
Acts 17:27-28 TPT

Our identity isn't found in what we do or what others say about us. Our identity is in Him and who He says we are. It's worth reading and studying His Word to find out who our creator says we are.

One of my favorite scriptures says I'm a child of God (see John 1:12). Since God is also referred to as the King of the universe, that makes us children of the King and joint heirs with Jesus (see Romans 8:17).

Purple is the color of royalty; no wonder we are drawn to the royal purple iris. It's a reminder of our Heavenly Father, the King of the Universe.

(Original post June 2023)

June
~ 4 ~

The heat has been dialed back a little, turning the world into a much more pleasant place. Years ago, when my in-laws first farmed, they had a small dairy here. Since dairies are typically named, they named it Pleasant Place Farm. I love that they chose that name. It was well-fitting then and still is now.

What we call things and people is important. God, who made us in His image, created the world with words. He called out: *"Let there be…"* and followed with *"It was very good."* Thankfully, He didn't say it was evil or stupid (see Genesis chapters 1 and 2).

Some may doubt that our words are important, but they are. Anyone who has worked with children has seen the impact that words have on little ones. Our words matter, and we have to choose them carefully.

Death and life are in the power of the tongue: And they
that love it shall eat the fruit thereof.
Proverbs 18:21

Jesus also talked about the importance of our words. In the book of Matthew, His words are recorded as:

But I say unto you, That every idle word that men shall speak, they shall
give account thereof in the day of judgment. For by thy words thou
shalt be justified, and by thy words thou shalt be condemned.
Matthew 12:36-37

I have driven by a run-down, dilapidated farm with the name Poverty Point displayed on the barn. And so it is. I'm glad the label given by Mark's parents spoke life and peace over our farm instead of death.

(Original post June 2023)

June
~ 5 ~

*T*he time for pink peonies has arrived. My red ones are diminishing as if making way for the beautiful pinks. Their reigns only overlap a little. It reminds me of a statement made by John the Baptist as some of his followers left him to follow Jesus:

He must increase, but I must decrease.
John 3:30

John could have been jealous or angry that his crowds were shrinking as Jesus' were growing, but he knew his place. He knew he wasn't the Christ and that Jesus, his cousin, was. He said what the cry of all believers' hearts should be, *"More of Jesus, less of me."*

When the disciples moved beyond themselves and were filled with the Holy Spirit, the power of God moved mightily through them, particularly Peter as he spoke and people experienced a move of God, not a move of Peter (see Acts 2). The same man who had denied knowing Christ was now boldly declaring Him. Peter had decreased. Christ had increased.

It's time to decrease and let the Lord reign in our hearts and lives. I must decrease and Christ must increase in me. It's time for a move of God.

(Original post June 2023)

June
~ 6 ~

*W*hat a difference a day makes! What a joy to have the sun return and light up our sky. There's a day I'm looking forward to when the Son will do the same.

And when he had spoken these things, while they beheld, he was taken up; and a cloud received him out of their sight. And while they looked steadfastly toward heaven as he went up, behold, two men stood by them in white apparel; which also said, Ye men of Galilee, why stand ye gazing up into heaven? This same Jesus, which is taken up from you into heaven, shall so come in like manner as ye have seen him go into heaven.
Acts 1:9-11

Jesus, speaking of his return, said:

For as the lightning cometh out of the east, and shineth even unto the west; so shall also the coming of the Son of man be.
Matthew 24:27

Instead of being born in a stable this time, He will make quite the entrance. The first time Jesus came, the people were expecting Him to come like a lion and be the conquering Messiah, but He came as a sacrificial lamb. Some are looking for the lamb to return, but I'm looking for the Lion of the Tribe of Judah.

The disciples thought Jesus would return in their lifetimes. Whenever they crested a hill, I'm guessing they were looking up, hoping to see Him. The day is certainly closer now than it was then. Will we see it? Maybe. Keep looking and live ready.

(Original post June 2022)

June
~ 7 ~

As I was finishing my post the other day, I caught a movement out of the corner of my eye. I looked up to see two cute little rabbits playing in the yard. They were hopping around, almost jumping over each other in their tag-like antics. They looked so cute and innocent, but I've had rabbits before; destruction was in their aftermath. Two young flowering trees died as a result of rabbits eating their bark. Likewise, when temptation presents itself, it doesn't show the end results of destruction and death. It shows up as innocent and fun.

Scripture even says there is pleasure in sin for a season (see Hebrews 11:4). But the season of pleasure eventually comes to an end, and the consequence of our choice comes.

For the wages of sin is death...
Romans 6:23a

Following tempting rabbit trails leads down paths of death of relationships. How many marriages die as a result of rabbit trails of porn and infidelity? Rabbit trails turned into addictions destroy health and wellness. Rabbit trails of wrong thinking undermine long-term happiness and joy. They all lead us away from our loving Father and into the grip of an evil taskmaster.

Thankfully, we have a God who restores and forgives. But He also leads and guides. If we pay attention to the red flags He gives us, we will avoid the paths that may look fun but lead to destruction. He isn't trying to block our fun. He knows the end game and is protecting our future. Yet He gives us the choice.

I call heaven and earth to record this day against you, that I have set before
you life and death, blessing and cursing: therefore choose life,
that both thou and thy seed may live.
Deuteronomy 30:19

Choose wisely.

(Original post June 2023)

June
~ 8 ~

A nest full of eggs is hidden amongst the begonias in a hanging basket on the front porch. When mama bird is off finding food, or whatever mama birds do, the leafy begonia provides a protective covering. Coverings are important, or else the eggs, and later baby birds, would be exposed to danger.

Prayer covering is also important . Praying prayers of faith over those we love isn't just a last resort when trouble hits. It is preemptive. Psalm 91 is one of my favorite scriptures to pray. These verses especially pertain to protection. I personalize them by inserting the name or names of whom I am praying for in the place of "thees" and "thous": *"Surely he shall deliver thee (insert name) from the snare of the fowler, and from the noisome pestilence. He shall cover thee (name) with his feathers, and under his wings shalt thou trust: His truth shall be thy shield and buckler." (Psalm 91:3-4).*

The snare of the fowler was a trap used to catch birds. Pestilence refers to sickness, especially plagues. I love the visual imagery this Psalm provides. I see our Protector's covering feathers and strong wings forming an iron dome covering as we pray.

(Original post June 2023)

June

~ 9 ~

*A*s some noticed in yesterday's post, a cowbird egg is in the nest among the others. I hadn't heard of cowbirds until I read the comments, so I did some research about them.

Basically, cowbirds are lazy and, instead of laying eggs in their own nest, they lay them in other birds' nests and leave the responsibility of incubation and nurturing to others. They are freeloaders. This information made me wonder: do I have freeloader-thought eggs laid in the nest of my mind that I am incubating? Did the intruder lay thoughts that, when grown, lead to stolen peace or a life devoid of joy? Am I sitting on eggs of jealousy or prejudice?

I need to examine the eggs I'm incubating. Not all thoughts that come through the window of our minds are ours. Sometimes, the enemy may drop an idea through someone's comment or, seemingly, out of nowhere. We are given good advice in Proverbs:

> *Guard your heart above all else, for it determines the course of your life.*
> *Proverbs 4:23 NLT*

The heart refers to the mind, will, and emotions. We are to guard our hearts and not nurture wayward thoughts. We are to rid our nests of intruder eggs, and only brood on thoughts that will be healthy and beneficial. Paul lists these types of thoughts for us:

> *Finally, brethren, whatsoever things are true, whatsoever things are honest, whatsoever things are just, whatsoever things are pure, whatsoever things are lovely, whatsoever things are of good report; if there be any virtue, and if there be any praise, think on these things.*
> *Philippians 4:8*

They are eggs worth incubating.

(Original post June 2023)

June
~ 10 ~

*T*here was one small strip of cloudless northeastern sky to peek through, and I could see a slice of bright, dark-red sunrise through it. The muted orange/pink sun in the photo doesn't even come close to the vivid reds I saw. Several attempts all provided the same disappointing dull shades, and editing was of no help.

There are times when our attempt to express a thought is limited. We can't capture in words the beauty of the moment or the awe in our hearts. How do you describe times spent in His presence? After Paul experienced glimpses of heaven, he expressed:

> *... I was caught up to paradise and heard things so astounding*
> *that they cannot be expressed in words...*
> 2 Corinthians 12:4 NLT

Yet those times of wonder bring us a surety of knowing through our own personal experience. I love God's Word, and we're to study it diligently. But we're also to experience life as a new creature in Christ.

When you've seen a seemingly hopeless person come to Jesus and their life does a 180° turn, you know it's possible. When you've seen healings occur before your eyes, you know Jesus still heals. When you have experienced *".... God's peace, which exceeds anything we can understand...."* (see Philippians 4:7, NLT), you know that even in the thick of life you are held secure by mighty hands. The person who has 'been there and experienced that' can't be dissuaded by a person with an argument against it. Our God calls us into a life of experience with Him:

> *O taste and see that the LORD is good: Blessed is the man that trusteth in him.*
> Psalm 34:8

Taste is active. It's experiential. It isn't passive waiting for a professional taster to describe their experience. We're to open wide and taste His goodness. It may result in wonders too glorious to describe.

(Original post June 2023)

June
~ 11 ~

This verse popped up in my memories from a couple of years ago:

Lord, if you measured us and marked us with our sins, who would ever have their prayers answered? But your forgiving love is what makes you so wonderful. No wonder you are loved and worshiped! This is why I wait upon you, expecting your breakthrough, for your word brings me hope.
Psalms 130:3-5 TPT

It made me think—if He measured us, none of us would measure up. Instead, He covered us with His righteous blood, and through it we stand tall. I love how the the verse continues; *You are loved and worshiped*, and *Your Word gives us hope* that a breakthrough is around the corner.

What an uplifting verse! It is a good one to think on throughout the day.

(Original post June 2022)

June
~ 12 ~

Thou preparest a table before me in the presence of mine enemies:
thou anointest my head with oil; my cup runneth over.
Psalm 23:5

He prepares a table for us; He provides for our needs. Even if I feel surrounded, I have a table of delight in His presence if I choose to take a seat. There, He anoints my head with healing oil. The head where thoughts can run wild is where the oil is applied, settling my soul in His presence.

I can get too busy. I can be preoccupied. But sitting a while at His table in the presence of the Lord is restful, and my soul finds strength and help in time of need right here at my place at His table.

(Original post June 2022)

June
~ 13 ~

I love it when the sun illuminates the east side of my house, and everything is suddenly brighter. Colors come to life when kissed with the morning sun.

We can pray a prayer to receive Jesus into our lives and thus become Christians, but still live in the shadows of darkness. We can be born again but refuse to grow up in the things of God. The difference is whether we received Jesus as Savior or as Lord. Did we ask Him into our lives as fire insurance against eternal flames, or do we live to serve Him? Are we self-centered or God-centered? Do we ignore His book, or do we love and study it to hear His voice and seek His will? Is our lifestyle the same after we prayed the prayer, or are we a new creation in Christ (see 2 Corinthians 5:17)?

Jesus said we're to *"make disciples of all nations"* (see Matthew 28:19). He didn't say to make converts. Converts pray the prayer and continue dwelling in the shadows of an unregenerated life. Disciples go on to live Son-kissed lives, illuminating His light to the world.

(Original post June 2023)

June
~ 14 ~

Today's Bible study and prayer time were moved inside. My recliner with Winnie on my lap won out over my outdoor glider.

It's Vacation Bible School time at my church. Tonight is the last night, and putting my feet up feels good. I help with the little itty-bitty kids. They are cuter than cute and faster than fast. Each one is individually fashioned in His image, complete with individual personalities, emotions, and eternal spirit.

What a blessing to teach God's Word to them. What a joy to experience their enthusiasm as they sing and complete crafts. Their comments are fun. Their prayers are sweet. Their smiles and hugs far outweigh the consequences of tired feet.

Jesus said, Suffer little children, and forbid them not, to come unto me: for of such is the kingdom of heaven. And he laid hands on them.
Matthew 19:14-15a

Jesus welcomed children. Previously, I hadn't noticed verse 15a: *"And He laid hands on them."* That means He put His hands on each one and blessed them. That's our prayer for each child—that each one will be touched and blessed by the Savior.

(Original post June 2023)

29

June
~ 15 ~

$\mathcal{I}$'m thankful for the large trees in my yard, which give shade to play and keep my house cool throughout hot summers. This one, in particular, is a favorite.

Years ago when my in-laws lived here, my husband and his brother used a few boards to build a tree house in this tree. A generation later, my boys climbed up to enjoy imaginary adventures. Over the years, the tree has grown, the boards used for steps have fallen off, and only one rickety board remains. The current generation of tree climbers has moved on to smaller trees but occasionally ask to hear stories of when their dads and grandpa played in its branches. The tree has become a legacy.

Our lives as believers are also to become legacy. Our experience with the Lord and the lessons we learn as we climb to higher and higher heights in Him are to provide an unshakable structure on which those coming behind can build.

Long ago, our youth group used to sing a song based on Psalm 1:1-3, which compares the life of a person who loves God and His Word to a mighty tree. We loudly chorused a recurrent line: *"Just like a tree planted by the waters, I will not be moved."*

Trees don't move. Their roots go down deep and remain unshakable by contrary storm winds. We are to be the tree providing structure and safety for future generations. Our heritage roots must go deep in the rich soil of God's Word. Our branches provide a strong and steady example to inspire future generations of tree climbers to build on.

(Original post June 2023)

June
~ 16 ~

The porch railings had become covered with a thick layer of dust, so I used a dry rag to dust them off yesterday. It was super easy to wipe the accumulation off the top rail, but it was a bit more difficult on the bottom as there were spindles to go around. Yet, without much effort, the railing returned to white except for a few areas, like on the post where the boards are rough and the dust is stuck in the crevices. A good wipe-down was ineffective. Hopefully, a scrub brush and soapy water will do the trick.

We all have rough spots, vulnerable areas where the dust of past hurts and sins has accumulated and isn't easily brushed off. To return our hot spots to their original pristine condition, they need to be cleansed by washing with water of the Word (see Ephesians 5:26).

God's Word shows us who God has called us to be. It heals our hearts, gives us grace to forgive, and sands off our rough spots. But we must know what it says and apply it to our lives before it can start the restorative washing of our hearts.

Some only use the Word to identify rough spots, but more importantly, it provides the solution for them. David's desire to be cleansed from the accumulated heavy dust of sin is recorded in the Psalms. He knew who to turn to for help:

Purify me from my sins, and I will be clean;
wash me, and I will be whiter than snow.
Psalms 51:7 NLT

His washing restores us. I hope to restore my porch posts to snow-colored white as well.

(Original post June 2023)

June
~ 17 ~

*I*t's lily time again! A friend gave me lily plants a few years ago, and I planted them in a shady area where little else of beauty has survived. They are in the shadow of tall pines, preventing them from getting much sunlight or water. Yet they reward me with bright blooms each year. Lilies must be hardy. Jesus uses them for an object lesson about not worrying about our daily provision. In days of high inflation, it's a good lesson to revisit.

Consider the lilies how they grow: they toil not, they spin not; and yet I say unto you, that Solomon in all his glory was not arrayed like one of these. If then God so clothe the grass, which is today in the field, and tomorrow is cast into the oven; how much more will he clothe you, O ye of little faith?
Luke 12:27-28

Jesus isn't saying to quit our jobs and pray to the god of the mailbox to send checks. I've known people who tried that. The point is to trust God and leave the worry behind.

Casting all your care upon him; for he careth for you.
1 Peter 5:7

Casting means to throw, and when you throw something, it's no longer with you. You have thrown it away. Instead of throwing away our cares, many of us cast them like a fisherman. They may go far from us, but then we reel them back in.

Our Father loves us. He will care for our needs. Worry never can. Let it go. Give it a good toss. Consider the lilies; how much more will He clothe you?

(Original post June 2023)

June
~ 18 ~

There is a note on my door today. Vivian, my 3-year-old granddaughter, was here yesterday and decided we should write a note warning bees to stay out. So our sign read: *"No bees allowed in grandma's house."* She said we should put it on the door. So we did. I asked her if bees could read. She said no, but the sign went up anyway and now I'm prepared for bees that attempt to enter, at least those that can read and follow signs.

Often, signs go unnoticed or unread. We blow past them unheeded by their warnings and then we are met with the fly swatters of life. We know that if we borrow more than we can pay back, the interest will eat us alive, yet credit cards become maxed out at high interest rates because shiny things outcry common sense. Intellect tells us children need our attention, but social media steals precious nuances, and their delightful stories fall on deaf ears. Examples are endless. We easily ignore the red warning signs that appear in our hearts as we speed past.

Unfortunately, receiving Jesus into our lives doesn't necessarily result in better heeding of warning signs, even though Jesus said to His disciples:

> *Behold, I send you forth as sheep in the midst of wolves: be ye*
> *therefore wise as serpents, and harmless as doves.*
> Matthew 10:16

This scripture implies that we are to be shrewd and innocent in our decision-making. Shrewd doesn't imply being wicked. According to Google, it means *"showing sharp powers of judgment."* People who notice and heed warnings are using good judgment.

The Holy Spirit is the writer who posts warning notes on our hearts. Our decisions will be wiser if we read and follow the signs.

(Original post June 2023)

June
~ 19 ~

*B*y the time I reached the front porch at 7:30 this morning, the sun was already high in the sky. Sleep was a battle last night. I simply could not stay asleep, so I allowed myself the luxury of sleeping in a bit and missed the sunrise. I also missed the quiet stillness of the early morning before birds make a racket and trucks and tractors come to life. I've learned to love that time of day when stillness transcribes into peace, and the sunrise kisses the horizon.

> *Be still, and know that I am God: I will be exalted among the heathen,*
> *I will be exalted in the earth.*
> *Psalm 46:10*

In our busy, sometimes chaotic lives, peace can be a rare commodity. I think of David, the psalmist, watching over his sheep as he mused on how the Lord was his shepherd. Distractions were minimal, allowing for more reflective thoughts as he meditated on his relationship with the Lord.

Be still, take a breath of the air He provided. In the stillness, know Him as creator God and be filled with wonder. For He will be exalted, raised up in praise by all the earth. Our stillness and pondering lead to praise, which may not be still at all.

Have a wonderful day. I hope it includes some peaceful moments.

(Original post June 2023)

June
~ 20 ~

*T*he irrigation is gracefully dancing across the field today, watering the thirsty crops. They need moisture regularly.

We were designed similarly. Being a believer isn't a one-and-done deal. We don't come to Jesus in one emotional encounter, make a faith confession, and then go on our merry way. Our need for the Lord is constant. As the old hymn says: *"I need thee every hour."*

David, referring to his great need for God, expressed it this way:

> *As the deer panteth after the water brooks, So panteth my soul after thee,*
> *O God. My soul thirsteth for God, for the living God...*
> *Psalm 42:1-2*

I'm thirsty again today, Lord. I will drink deeply from the river of living water and find satisfaction in You alone.

(Original post June 2022)

41

June
~ 21 ~

*T*he sun was a bright red ball of fire when it first made its appearance this morning, but you'd never know from the photos on my phone. Even this enhanced one doesn't show forth the true colors. Sometimes, you just need to be there in person.

Looking back through old photos brings up memories; sometimes happy and sometimes bittersweet. Sharing them with others who weren't there gives a glimpse but it's not the same as reliving it with someone who experienced the event with you. Knowing the story by experience is much richer and broader than knowing it through someone else's experience, even if they share the enhanced version.

We must build our own story with the Lord and not try to live vicariously through someone else's experience. We have the opportunity to invite Him into each of our days.

O taste and see that the LORD is good...
Psalm 34:8a

We each get to taste His goodness, which needs no enhancements.

(Original post June 2023)

June

~ 22 ~

There's a gentle breeze on the porch this morning. It feels wonderful. I'm trying to soak it in before the day's heat comes. I could linger in this pleasantness forever.

Psalm 63 begins with these words: *"O God, thou art My God; early will I seek thee: My soul thirsteth for thee..."* The coolness will give way, and the heat of the day will come, but the early times in the morning set the tone for the day.

(Original post June 2022)

June

~ 23 ~

*I*t is a still morning on the farm. Nothing is stirring. Since it's supposed to rain today, I've placed my hanging baskets and other plants where they will receive the benefits. It's been dry for so long they are all covered in dust. A good washing will spruce them up.

In dry spells, we long for rain. In times when the heavens seem brass and prayers don't seem to break through, we long for the Holy Spirit to rain down on us. In those times, I've positioned myself to receive the rain. I've prayed the prayer David recorded in Psalm 139:23-24:

> *Search me, O God, and know my heart: Try me, and know my thoughts: And see if there be any wicked way in me, And lead me in the way everlasting.*

I also made sure I didn't miss opportunities to gather with other believers at church and in small group Bible studies. Prayers to set my heart right prepared me to receive, and gathering with other believers also put me in the right place to receive. Breakthroughs always come when I pray with others. It's where the Holy Spirit has rained down.

It's Sunday, a great day for the dust of life to be washed off. It will spruce us up again.

(Original post June 2023)

June
~ 24 ~

$\mathcal{S}$unrise put on a show this morning. Starting at 6:00 a.m., the sky was aflame for the following 20 minutes with shades of pinks, oranges, and blues. I took over 30 pictures of the ever-changing mixture and blending of colors. What a gorgeous start to my day. It made it easier to declare *"Good morning, Lord!"* instead of *"Good Lord, it's morning."*

The psalmist often writes of sunrises and sunsets:

O God, to the farthest corners of the planet people will stand in awe, startled
and stunned by your signs and wonders. Sunrise brilliance and sunset
beauty both take turns singing their songs of joy to you.
Psalm 65:8 TPT

I like the word picture of the sunrise and sunset singing praise to their creator. It seems like just an analogy, but in recent years studies have been done on sounds in space. Although it was long thought that space was devoid of sound, studies by space Scientists have found sound in space. There are conditions in the thin atmosphere causing sounds to be emitted below the lowest sounds we can hear. Perhaps somehow, when sunrays meet the horizon, a celestial song of praise arises.

Whether the sky rejoices or not is not my responsibility; my daily attitude and praise levels are. Psalm 113:3 spells it out clearly:

From the rising of the sun unto the going down of the same,
the LORD's name is to be praised.

The Passion Translation states it as:

From sunrise-brilliance to sunset-beauty, lift up his praise from dawn to dusk!

The sun is up. So it's time. Let the praises begin.

(Original post June 2023)

June

~ 25 ~

$\mathcal{W}$henever I type the current date, I double-check my calendar app to make sure I get it right. Today, the app displays it's the 28th. I'm not sure how it skipped from the 25th to the 28th. I don't understand how automated things go haywire, or how to fix them. So, part of my day will be figuring it out. I can either be irritated or see it as an opportunity to learn new things.

My default with technology is the irritation route. But being irritated won't solve it, so I'm choosing to believe Philippians 4:13 which states: *"I can do all things through Christ which strengtheneth me."* And I'll pray for guidance, lots of guidance. I'm guessing that Google or YouTube will have some suggestions. The school of life is full of unintended lessons.

Counting it all joy today (see James 1:2) may have me taking several counting-to-10 breaks. Hopefully, the calendar will be back on the right day tomorrow.

(Original post June 2022)

June
~ 26 ~

Seventy-five years ago today, my parents were married. Mom's dress was a beautiful, heavy satin and lace gown with satin buttons and long train. She wore it on what she said was a very hot day. Oh, and of course they didn't benefit from an air-conditioned church, so that was just how it was. I'm sure Dad, in a double-breasted suit, wasn't any cooler. Their marriage lasted until Dad's death in 1996. They modeled a marriage of love.

Their home was a safe haven for my brother and me and my grandmother, who lived with us for seven years. Family and neighbors were almost always dropping by, as the door was always open. There rarely was a night that Dad didn't make sticky popcorn, much like a popcorn ball that wasn't formed into a ball. He called it cracker-jack, and it was amazingly good.

In the winter, we took turns turning the crank to make homemade ice cream. Days were full of hard work on the farm. Mom, who had grown up using horses, had said she'd never marry a farmer. But she happily drove tractors and combines alongside Dad. Often, nights were spent with neighbors around the table playing cards. Cousins came for weeks at a time to share farm life. It was a great life.

Today, after 27 anniversaries apart, they are together again. Today, I'm thankful for legacy. I'm thankful for heaven. I'm thankful they knew Jesus and He welcomed them home when their lives ended. I'm thankful they are together, and goodbye was not forever.

(Original post June 2023)

The last couple of days of rain have been amazing. The grass has already started to turn from brown to green. The fields are soaking it in. Behind the row of tractors is an irrigation system which was still running at the time I took this photo, even though it had begun to rain hard. Why? Because after a couple of months of being devoid of rain, the ground was extremely dry. At that point, the beets needed more moisture than the little rain we had gotten provided, so the irrigation system was left to run its course.

Sometimes we stop early. At the beginning of a move of God, as we begin to see the rain of the Holy Spirit, we can get lost in the excitement and stop praying. We can settle when we need to continue to press. It's exciting to feel the goosebumps and the awe of His presence, but it's not to end there. We are to carry His presence to others. We're to press in through our prayers to see the mercy of the Lord reach those around us.

Before Jesus ascended, He told His disciples and others to wait for the promise of the Father. They gathered in an upper room where they waited and prayed for 40 days. Then it happened:

And suddenly there came a sound from heaven as of a rushing mighty wind,
and it filled all the house where they were sitting.
Acts 2:2

They didn't settle for the wind of the experience. As revealed in the rest of the chapter, they were filled with the Holy Spirit, spoke in languages they didn't know, and took to the streets. They were changed. Men who cowered in fear days before were boldly declaring the truth that Jesus was the Messiah. He had died and had risen from the dead. Some laughed at them, but approximately 3,000 were baptized that day and came into the kingdom. The disciples didn't settle for the goosebumps at the beginning of the rain. They pressed in and turned the world right-side up. It's our turn.

(Original post June 2023)

June
~ 28 ~

I took my hanging flowers down during the rains and put them where they would get more rain...that is, all but this one. I'd taken it down briefly, but there was a nest inside packed with baby birds, and the little mama Finch couldn't find it. I watched her perched on the railing below where it usually was hanging, franticly searching for the plant I thought I'd placed in plain sight for her to find. So back up it went. While the other five were basking in luxurious rain drops, this one stoically stayed in its place. Mama Finch was happy again. When her babies were missing, she couldn't keep them safe under her wing, as mama birds do.

Sometimes, we get caught up in the circumstances of life and find ourselves moved away from where we belong. Storms have come, and our thoughts are not where they should be. It's time to move back to the protective covering of the Lord. The 91st Psalm is a reassurance of God's love and care for us. Verse four compares His protection to a mother bird's protective wings:

> *He shall cover thee with his feathers, and under his wings shalt thou trust:*
> *His truth shall be thy shield and buckler.*
> *Psalm 91:4*

But the forerunning verses lay down some parameters. They speak of dwelling in the secret place of the most high and abiding under His shadow. Both imply close proximity. Mama bird's wings only cover the little birdies that are close. And that's where I figuratively want to be, walking in His shadow, safely sheltered in His presence.

(Original(Original post June 2023)

June
~ 29 ~

*T*his little flower was unexpected. I didn't know the hanging vines that came with my geraniums would flower, too. It was a surprise, a small bonus flower that could have been overlooked.

Sometimes blessings are like that. They show up unexpectedly and go unacknowledged. I need to notice the good things along the way.

Every good gift and every perfect gift is from above, and cometh down from the Father of lights, with whom is no variableness, neither shadow of turning.
James 1:17

When gifts are given, it's rude to not acknowledge them and thank the giver. Thank you, Lord, for Your unexpected blessings. Forgive me for not noticing or thanking You for blessings, especially those I wasn't expecting.

(Original post June 2022)

June

~ 30 ~

The daisies are about to have their day in the sun as their season is upon us. I love their simple beauty. Somehow, daisies seem like happy flowers. They make me smile. They are like the simple pleasures of life.

Sometimes, the value of simplicity can pass us by. Sometimes, we focus more on the more elegant rose-like experiences and take little notice of the everyday simple pleasures of family life; a child's giggle, a warm greeting, hug or dinnertime conversation with your spouse, or the daisies in your life that cause your lips to turn upward in a smile.

The special times of vacations or celebrations and the roses of life are also important, even though more infrequent. Focusing instead on the "daisies" brings day-to-day joy. It also makes being continuously thankful easier to accomplish (see 1Thessalonians 5:16-18).

Keeping our focus on small daily blessings instead of little annoyances makes a big difference in our attitude and behavior. If we take note of the blessings, by the end of the day, we'll have gathered a beautiful bouquet of daisies, and we will have had a good day. A good day indeed.

(Original post June 2023)

I could linger in this pleasantness forever.
~Jeanne Chaffin

July
2024

July
~ 1 ~

Translucent mushrooms, or toadstools, were in front of my front porch this morning. Since they weren't there yesterday, they seem to have appeared out of nowhere. Yet, even these here-today-gone-tomorrow fungi are beautifully designed.

Nature is full of beauty, be it in the distinct patterns on a butterfly's wing, the magnificence of a mighty redwood, or a delicate pattern in a translucent mushroom, each demonstrates design, and designs come from designers. Nature was designed and created by a masterful creator.

As the scripture tells us:

In the beginning, God created the heaven and the earth.
Genesis 1:1

That's why we often feel closer to God when we're in nature. God didn't just design nature, He also designed us unique with our own pattern of DNA and fingerprints, giftings and abilities, and each uniquely loved and called by the designer Himself. We can trust in Him.

(Original post July 2023)

July

~ 2 ~

The cloudy skies must have suppressed the birds' wild songs this morning; they are relatively quiet. The stillness reminds me of a scripture verse:

Be still, and know that I am God; I will be exalted among
the nations, I will be exalted in the earth.
Psalms 46:10

Be still... don't question. Be still... drop the "what ifs," and the "whys." Quiet the raging mind. Be still and know He is God.

He's God, and I'm not. I can come to Him in prayer. I can cast my cares on Him (see 1 Peter 5:7), but sometimes I need just to come—not ask, not talk, just come. I need to be still and know. I can rest in His presence as a child with its head resting on its father's chest.

In our world of constant noise, how refreshing it is to be still. How comforting it is to know.

(Original post July 2022)

July

~ 3 ~

It's the time of year when even weeds are beautiful. Visiting the ditch with a grandson afforded me the view of this milkweed decked out in pink blooms, and on its right, some wild carrots, sometimes called Queen Anne's Lace.

As a kid, I hoed them out of my dad's navy bean fields since weeds rob bean plants of water and nutrients, thus diminishing yields. Yet, they decorate ditches and roadsides beautifully and attract butterflies.

He has made everything beautiful in its time. Also, he has put eternity into man's heart, yet so that he cannot find out what God has done from the beginning to the end.
Ecclesiastes 3:11 ESV

He makes even weeds beautiful. He also puts the wonder of eternity in our hearts to ponder the things of God. That verse continues by stating we'll never figure it all out but it intrigues us, and we find the more we learn, the more there is yet to learn. Our minds cannot understand all there is to know about Him.

Such knowledge is too wonderful for me; It is high, I cannot attain unto it.
Psalm 139:6

If He can turn weeds into works of art, imagine what He can do with us when we submit our lives to Him. We can go from weeds to masterpieces, from rebelliously selfish, doing our own thing even if it steals nutrients from others, to obedient people of faith caring for others.

He can make all things new, even me.

(Original post July 2023)

July
~ 4 ~

Independence Day

$\mathcal{T}$he sun is rising beautifully on this holiday morning. What a glorious day to celebrate our nation's founding.

While sitting on the front porch, as I typed that last sentence, there was a commotion of flapping wings in a nearby pine tree. Suddenly, a large bird, perhaps a hawk, chased a much smaller one out of the tree and toward me. The larger one came close enough that I felt the breeze as he went by in pursuit. The little bird dove into a bush, and the larger one took flight.

I hadn't seen birds of prey or fights for survival in the yard before. It all happened quickly, too fast to get a photo. Then it was over, and peace again reigned.

I'm thankful for peace in our nation and in my heart, which only the Lord can give, for He is the Prince of Peace (see Isaiah 9:6).

Happy 4th of July! Happy birthday, America!

(Original post July 2023)

July
~ 5 ~

My grandson, an excellent toad catcher, visited the farm the other day. He helped with many tasks; deadheading flowers, eradicating weeds, and watering flowers. It was the latter when he noticed movement, and the toad catcher extraordinaire jumped into action. He quickly laid aside the hose and cupped his hands, preparing to capture the little guy. If he had continued to hold tightly to the hose, the prize toad would have escaped his grasp.

To capture all that the Lord has for us, we need to lay down the things that hold us back. Jesus made this point with a word picture saying:

> *The kingdom of heaven is like unto a merchant man, seeking goodly pearls:*
> *who, when he had found one pearl of great price, went and*
> *sold all that he had, and bought it.*
> *Matthew 13:45-46*

He laid down everything for the prize.

Paul tells of laying down his reputation and position, all he had for the prize of knowing Jesus:

> *It's true that I once relied on all that I had become. I had a reason to boast and impress people with my accomplishments—more than others—for my pedigree was impeccable. To truly know him meant letting go of everything from my past and throwing all my boasting on the garbage heap. It's all like a pile of manure to me now, so that I may be enriched in the reality of knowing Jesus Christ and embrace him as Lord in all of his greatness.*
> *Philippians 3:4, 8 TPT*

Am I holding onto something that prevents me from catching the prize of knowing and embracing Jesus as Lord? It's something to pray about. If God reveals that I am still clutching an old habit, thought pattern, self-sufficiency, etc., it's time to lay it down, jump into action, and prepare to capture my prize. It will be a pearl of great price, not a prize toad.

(Original post July 2023)

July
~ 6 ~

*T*his coral geranium was from last year. I kept it over the winter and have babied it all summer, watching for a hint of a bloom. Finally, it has rewarded me with a blossom.

Sometimes we must wait, which is challenging in an instant drive-thru society. We're used to fast food and instant answers from Google searches. Waiting seems to be a lost art. Yet the scriptures tell us *"...faith and patience inherent the promises"* (see Hebrews 12:2).

Patience implies a time factor is involved. We pray, we claim His promises, and we wait. We're to pray in faith and to wait with expectancy.

As a first-time mom prepares a room for a nursery and gathers baby supplies to be ready to welcome her newborn, we're to prepare to welcome our answer. During the waiting period, we incubate the answer, building our faith by meditating on the Word. Hens know enough to stay on the nest, incubating their eggs until the chicks hatch. So should we. Giving up early aborts the answer.

Hold tight. Don't throw in the towel or throw out the plant, which I almost did. Promises blossom for those who persist.

(Original post July 2023)

July
~ 7 ~

The dry weather, plus semi-trucks going around my circle drive and west winds blowing across fields, made for a perfect dust storm at my house, and my windows showed it. Washing them was pointless until the driveway was brined to hold down the dust. I was literally seeing through a glass darkly. But the day came when stones were brought in, the driveway was leveled and brined, so I finished washing the windows yesterday. What a remarkable difference it made.

> *For now we see through a glass, darkly; but then face to face: now I know in part; but then shall I know even as also I am known.*
> *1 Corinthians 13:12*

We don't have a complete understanding of the Lord and His Word in this life; we see through a glass darkly. Yet we're instructed to:

> *Study to shew thyself approved unto God, a workman that needeth not to be ashamed, rightly dividing the word of truth.*
> *2 Timothy 2:15*

As we study, we learn more of His truth, clearing peek holes in the proverbial dark glass so we can live better in His ways. As we seek, our view becomes clearer and clearer.

That's what He calls us to do: seek, study, listen, and obey. Today, I'm heading to church where my pastor will use a little Windex on another area of the window of my life so the light of the Gospel can shine through. What a difference it will make. See you there!

(Original post July 2023)

July
~ 8 ~

*T*he new day dawns, and life begins on the farm. Wheat is nearly ready to be harvested. Wheat harvesting is one of my favorite times of summer. It stirs up memories of my cousins coming to visit when we were kids. We played in the truck bed all afternoon, burying each other in the wheat as if it were sand at the beach. What fun childhood memories to cherish.

Thinking back on good times is a blessing. Thinking back on times of God's faithfulness builds our faith. When the Israelites were in the wilderness, they faced lack of water more than once. Instead of reminding themselves of how God supplied every time, and resting in the knowledge that He would do it again, they complained each time.

In Exodus, I read of their experiences and wonder why they didn't figure it out. Then life happens. Something comes up that I've faced before, and my first response is to worry instead of looking back on how God graciously answered in the past.

I have to purposely halt my thought pattern and remind myself of examples of the Lord's faithfulness in my life. I also search for scripture promises that relate to the current situation. Doing so builds my faith and gives me peace while waiting for answers.

He's the faithful God who does it again.

(Original post July 2022)

July
~ 9 ~

Since the rains were north of us yesterday, the irrigation system is still running this morning. Thirsty crops call for water. In dry years, the crops' roots go deep in search of moisture.

A sound root system is essential as it also provides strength and stability to the plant. In Colossians 2, we find:

Let your roots grow down into him, and let your lives be built on him.
Then your faith will grow strong in the truth you were taught,
and you will overflow with thankfulness.
Colossians 2:7 NLT

Letting our roots go down deep in the truth of His Word takes time, study, and thought. It is worth it to develop deep roots in Him instead of in the sands of worry. His Word is good soil, which produces the overflow of thankfulness.

(Original post July 2022)

July
~ 10 ~

*W*hat a beautiful sunrise this morning. I took several pictures as the sun quickly rose in the sky. I'm thankful I don't have to wait to have the film developed; I get to see the results instantly from my phone camera. But life isn't like that.

The consequences of our actions often take months, if not years, to fully develop, and we lose sight of the cause and effect. We dwell on negative thoughts, speak destructive words, and wonder why our relationships are broken.

We're instructed to think good thoughts (see Philippians 4:8) and speak the truth in love (see Ephesians 4:15).

> *Death and life are in the power of the tongue: And they*
> *that love it shall eat the fruit thereof.*
> *Proverbs 18:21*

One thought at a time and one word at a time; we give life or death to relationships. It's our mind. It's our voice. Choose wisely.

(Original post July 2022)

July
~ 11 ~

$\mathcal{D}$ark skies and a few small puddles welcomed me this morning. We didn't get much rain, but as dry as it's been, even a little is a blessing.

Israel spent 400 years in a drought of the Word of God between the Old and New Testaments. Malachi ends with the prophecy that Elijah would come before the day of the Lord. Four hundred dry years later, an old priest had an encounter with an angel while attending to his duties. He was informed that he and his barren wife would give birth to a child named John. It was a brief encounter, a seemingly little shower of God's Word. But the drought was broken.

We know this child as John the Baptist, who came in the spirit and power of Elijah. Four hundred years of silence, followed by a word to a priest, then a word to a young girl named Mary, and the world was about to be forever changed. God doesn't forget His promises. They come right on time.

> *But when the fulness of the time was come, God sent forth his Son,*
> *made of a woman, made under the law, to redeem them that*
> *were under the law, that we might receive the adoption of sons.*
> *Galatians 4:4-5*

Stay faithful to Him in the time of waiting. He's faithful to us.

(Original post July 2022)

July
~ 12 ~

*T*his is my typical morning spot, but today I'm in my recliner looking out the window instead. It's only 56°, pretty cool for a July morning, so I chose to stay inside.

It's amazing how much warmer 56° feels in the spring when it's been much colder, and how cool it feels following 80° days. Our experience shapes our perspective. Yet our Bibles tell us our experience isn't supposed to determine our worldview.

Paul's letter to the Roman church warns against conforming to popular opinion, stating:

> *And be not conformed to this world: but be ye transformed by the renewing of your mind, that ye may prove what is that good, and acceptable, and perfect, will of God."*
> Romans 12:2

We're not to fit into the mold of the world. We're to undergo a metamorphosis of how we think through the cocoon process of the Word of God. My perspective is to be God's perspective. I need to be shaped by His influence in my life. I need to filter my thoughts through His Word and thus renew my mind. His ways won't come naturally, as they are much grander than mine.

> *For my thoughts are not your thoughts, neither are your ways my ways, saith the LORD. For as the heavens are higher than the earth, so are my ways higher than your ways, and my thoughts than your thoughts.*
> Isaiah 55:8-9

His Word stretches me and challenges me to think differently, to think eternally instead of momentarily. It lifts me instead of pulling me down. I'm still in the process and have a long way to go. But I'm not where I was. Renewal takes time and persistence. Today's a good day to open the book, spend time with its author, and gain His thoughts and perspective.

(Original post July 2023)

July
~ 13 ~

*I*t's a sunrise over mud puddles type of day. The crops are benefiting from the intermittent showers we've experienced of late. It seemed after the rains came, everything grew by leaps and bounds. Gardens and fields that were watered took off after the rain.

You'd think water is water, but there is something about rain water that makes a difference in plant life. It reminds me of Jesus referring to Himself as the living water (see John 7). He didn't say He was the only water, but that He was the only life-giving water.

Jesus wasn't exclusionary. He called for the whosoevers (see Mark 8:34), but He did say He was the only living water source which makes Him controversial. He was then, and He is now. He didn't say I am one of many ways. He said I am the way (see John 14:6).

Early believers were referred to as people of the way. They chose to follow Jesus and drink from the water of life, and so do we.

(Original post July 2023)

July
~ 14 ~

I'm wrapped in my blanket this 45° morning, awaiting the sunrise. I won't wait long as the sun is quickly lighting the sky and changing the surrounding dark clouds to things of beauty.

When the angels appeared to the shepherds at the time of Jesus' birth, the shepherds experienced the light as the radiance of God's glory. Although momentarily terrified, they recovered and were encouraged to seek the Savior (see Luke 2).

When Saul saw the light on the road to Damascus, his life was forever changed as he went from persecutor to promoter of the Gospel. God's light causes us to seek, to change, and to reflect His light into the world.

We can all draw close to him with the veil removed from our faces. And with no veil we all become like mirrors who brightly reflect the glory of the Lord Jesus....
2 Corinthians 3:18 TPT

It's time to get ready for church. Worshipping together and hearing God's Word helps wash the spots off my mirror so I reflect the glory of the Lord better.

(Original post July 2022)

July

~ 15 ~

I met long-time friends for lunch here the other day, where the food is always good and the flowers are beautiful. Meeting with friends, talking, laughing, and reminiscing about Jesus stories together is so refreshing. And Bible study friends gathered around my table last night, sharing dinner while discussing God's Word, what it meant, and how to apply it. We talked, we laughed, we challenged each other, and we prayed together. We grew from each other's perspective and were encouraged and blessed. We had taken a few weeks off due to busy schedules, and getting back together felt great.

Community is important. We're not designed to go it alone:

And the LORD God said, 'It is not good that the man should be alone....'
Genesis 2:18a

Man being alone was the only deficiency in a perfect garden, so God remedied it. We need others for companionship and to challenge our way of thinking. In Proverbs we read:

As iron sharpens iron, so a friend sharpens a friend.
Proverbs 27:17 NLT

My thoughts may seem right to me, but friends often help stretch my understanding and sometimes show me the error of my ways. Without community, we can get weird. The year 2020 showed us our great need for others in our lives as the world lost touch and things got strangely weird. Gathering over meals, gathering for worship, or just for fun, is healthy.

And let us not neglect our meeting together, as some people do, but encourage one another, especially now that the day of his return is drawing near.
Hebrews 10:25 NLT

Take the time to spend time with your community. You'll be glad you did.

(Original post July 2023)

July
~ 16 ~

*I*t's a rainy morning, but I can sit in the shelter of the porch roof, listening to the pitter-patter of raindrops falling while I'm safe and dry. I'm reminded of a couple of scripture verses about God's protective shelter:

He shall cover thee with his feathers, and under his wings shalt thou trust:
His truth shall be thy shield and buckler.
Psalm 91:4

The name of the LORD is a strong tower: The righteous runneth into it, and is safe.
Proverbs 18:10

Both these analogies convey a similar concept: He supplies shelter, but we must run to it and stay underneath. It's easy to be the disobedient little chick doing our own thing instead of staying under His wing or inside His tower. The same lure of pride hooked Adam and Eve in the garden: *'Eat the apple, be like God,'* now appearing as *'I'll make my own truth and build a tower my own way.'*

God doesn't tell us to find our own way. Rather, He tells us to follow His way. It leads to towers of strength in His name and shelters under His mighty arms. Rainstorms will come. Shelters built on the rock of His truth are known to stand, while shelters resting on shifting sand are notorious for collapsing, leaving occupants out in the rain.

(Original post July 2023)

July

~ 17 ~

Arise, shine; for thy light is come, and the glory of the LORD is risen upon thee.
For, behold, the darkness shall cover the earth, and gross darkness the people:
but the LORD shall arise upon thee, and his glory shall be seen upon thee.
And the Gentiles shall come to thy light, and kings to the brightness of thy rising.
Isaiah 60:1-3

*E*arly this morning, the brilliant sun reminded me of the above scripture verses. Great hope comes from them. Although the world may be struggling with darkness, His light still arises for all to see, and unbelievers are still drawn to it.

Hope is vital. It keeps us moving forward when we want to give up. It reminds us of our dreams even when they seem covered in dark clouds of impossibilities. Hope gives us courage. When facing dark days of discouragement, grab onto hope and arise. Shine because your light is come. It *is* come; not it *might* come sometime in the future. It *is* present tense now.

Sometimes we need to act on our hopes to bring them to pass. Be full of joy. Be encouraged. Light is here. His glory is here. Shine.

(Original post July 2023)

July
~ 18 ~

*T*he hostas blooms are beginning with just a few. It doesn't seem like much, but many more will follow soon. It's a small beginning. Sometimes, we're discouraged when our beginnings aren't grandiose.

Regarding the rebuilding of the temple, Zechariah 4:10 says: *"Do not despise these small beginnings, for the Lord rejoices to see the work begin..."*

Our projects, careers, and ministry usually start small. Our educations begin with kindergarten not grad school. God's advice is to not be discouraged or give up; staying faithful in small things leads to being faithful in much.

God is faithful, and we need to be too. Thank God for small beginnings!

(Original post July 2023)

July
~ 19 ~

ℛecently, I was at a place where someone was turning an old dead tree into a work of art. The artist is obviously gifted in creating beauty out of what would be death. We know an artist like that who makes beauty out of ashes (see Isaiah 61:3).

We all have ashes, areas of our lives where dreams burned down and turned to ashes. We can't reconstruct them, but the master creator can. In the master's hand, our dreams will rise up in resurrected form, revised and stronger than before. The key is to allow the artist access to our dead "trees," and the process begins.

The Spirit of the Lord GOD is upon me; because the LORD hath anointed me to preach good tidings unto the meek; he hath sent me to bind up the brokenhearted, to proclaim liberty to the captives, and the opening of the prison to them that are bound; to proclaim the acceptable year of the LORD, and the day of vengeance of our God; to comfort all that mourn; to appoint unto them that mourn in Zion, to give unto them beauty for ashes, the oil of joy for mourning, the garment of praise for the spirit of heaviness; that they might be called trees of righteousness, the planting of the LORD, that he might be glorified.
Isaiah 61:1-3

(Original post July 2023)

July

~ 20 ~

My morning view never grows old. I am thankful to live in the country surrounded by growing crops and farm machinery.

The guys are starting early today, and the morning is anything but quiet. Yet, it's still my favorite place to be. It's peaceful even when it's not quiet. Sometimes, our lives are surrounded by outside noise, yet we can have peace within.

One of the titles for Jesus is the Prince of Peace (see Isaiah 9:6). Each Christmas we sing *"wonderful counselor, the Prince of Peace"* in the Hallelujah Chorus. Yet, it's more than lyrics in a song. He reigns in peace, bringing peace to troubled hearts. We simply have to turn to Him as He's always there. We also have to yield to Him.

When I faced the winds of grief, He directed me regarding what thoughts to dwell on and what thoughts to take captive. I didn't have to follow His lead, but I needed to if I wanted peace. It felt counterintuitive, but I'm thankful I followed, at least most of the time, because peace made the way ahead doable.

The peace of God is priceless and well worth the effort of taking stray thoughts under control.

(Original post July 2023)

July
~ 21 ~

*T*he sky was beautiful early last evening, with great sunlight peeking through clouds. The newly harvested wheat field with large square bales of straw in the foreground added a definitive July imprint, reminding me of Julys long past spent in the back of a wheat truck with my brother and cousins. We'd spend the hot afternoons using wheat like sand to bury each other as Dad harvested with a small tractor-pulled combine, and Mom drove the truck. We had great days.

I don't remember sunburns or arguments. I only remember happy times of being together without a care in the world. Of course, my memory is selective. I'm sure there were arguments, sunburns, and cares, but memories often idealize our life stories.

I'm glad the Bible doesn't do that. It gives us the good, the bad, and even the ugly side of people's lives. David's flaws weren't covered up in the pages of scripture. They are there for all to see. Jesus' great-great-great (and maybe a few more greats) Grandmother Rahab, who hid the spies in Jericho, was introduced to us as a prostitute. Before being the great deliverer, Moses murdered a man in Egypt. James and John were known for their horrible tempers. And the list goes on. Yet, all of them were used mightily by God. None were beyond His reach. None were thrown away as damaged goods, and neither are we.

He can work through our flaws and our inadequacies. We just need to be available and obedient. In so doing, He works through the pages of our lives to build His story of love and redemption. Our example may not be pristine, but it will show that God is still in the business of using ordinary people to do extraordinary things.

(Original post July 2023)

July

~ 22 ~

These are my cousin's hibiscus flowers. I used to have some similar to these by my front porch. Instead of Annie's beautiful yellow, mine were an amazing pink. They were a Mother's Day gift and meant a lot to me. The deer thought they were delicious. I don't eat venison, but I was tempted.

Loss hurts. When I returned from Annie's, somehow the lyrics of an old song came back and got stuck in my head. It was a song that reminded me of loss. I could hear Barbara Streisand's voice singing, *"You don't send me flowers anymore."* It went around and around in my mind. Mark loved sending me flowers, usually red roses, sometimes just one, sometimes a dozen. They came often. The song pulled at my emotions.

I also felt the red flag of the Holy Spirit as He whispered, *"Don't go there."* I was again reminded that Mark had been promoted to heaven.

For to me, to live is Christ, and to die is gain.
Philippians 1:21

Gain is promotion. He is fine. He is experiencing the glory of heaven. I was also reminded that the Lord is with me, and I'm fine with that, too. But how do you stop a thought, or worse, a looping song? I knew I had to interrupt it. Sometimes I do so by singing praise. This time, I grabbed my phone and brought up a YouTube video of a favorite pastor sharing the Word. My mind and emotions settled down. Peace returned, as did joy.

I knew the sadness would build if I didn't stop the sad song in my head. I also knew that the joy of the Lord is my strength (see Nehemiah 8:10). If I choose sadness, I will return to a world of hopelessness. The Holy Spirit alerted me to the fork in the road. But the choice was mine. I had to make the choice to encourage myself in the Lord (see 1 Samuel 30:6). Then the comfort of the Lord filled me again.

I have encouragement for those who have lost loved ones. Those we have lost who loved the Lord are not just in our past. They are part of our future, too. We'll be reunited in heaven. I have read reports that the flowers there are amazing. Perhaps there will be bouquets. If so, mine will be red roses that never fade.

(Original post July 2022)

July
~ 23 ~

I have a small apple tree which produces Macintosh apples in the fall. But with the strong winds of late, I've been finding small apples all over the ground. Each fallen apple will never reach its purpose—which in my world is to turn into yummy applesauce or apple pie. Each of us has a divine purpose. *"I know the plans I have for you saith the Lord…"* (see Jeremiah 29:11). To reach it we need to stay connected to our life source.

As recorded in John 15:5, Jesus said: *"I am the vine, you are the branches if you remain in me you will bear much fruit."* The apples that dropped during the storm are underdeveloped, bitter, and good for nothing. I don't want to share their fate. They serve as a good reminder to hold on to the One who will never leave or forsake us (see Hebrews 13:5).

Staying connected lets the fruit of the spirit, which is sweet as pie, mature in us. The spirit fruit is detailed in Galatians 5:22-23:

> *But the fruit of the Spirit is love, joy, peace, longsuffering, gentleness, goodness, faith, meekness, temperance: against such there is no law.*

Storms won't last forever; outlast the storm, be fruitful.

(Original post July 2022)

$\mathcal{I}$ love the broad leaves of hosta plants. They cover the ground with their vibrant green. I had a protective covering on my knee a while back, which wasn't vibrant or majestic. I'd fallen off my bike and ripped an area of skin off, and for a couple of weeks I had an ugly scab covering the sore until new skin grew. Bodies get hurt sometimes and need to go through the healing process. It's not a pretty time, but thank God for it, or I'd be one large Band-Aid.

God calls the church 'His body.' At times, there are hurts and "knees" get ripped up in our church body and need to be healed. When there are disputes between members, there is a process for healing. Jesus said:

> *So if you are presenting a sacrifice at the altar in the Temple and you suddenly remember that someone has something against you, leave your sacrifice there at the altar. Go and be reconciled to that person.*
> *Then come and offer your sacrifice to God.*
> *Matthew 5:23-24 NLT*

The sacrifice to God becomes secondary to a restored relationship. Reconciliation may be painful, takes prayer, and at times, help from others as the wound scabs over. But if this process is followed, new skin - pink and vibrant - is formed.

Breaks in relationships can tug at heartstrings to pull us back from taking risks on new hurts, but knees and relationships both heal with God's help. It's time to get back on our bike and ride.

(Original post July 2023)

July
~ 25 ~

Today, my life returns to normal. We're back from our family vacation and I'm back to front-porch-mornings. I used to be sad at returning to normal, but somewhere over time, I learned to appreciate my normal everyday life and routines. There really is no place like home.

Following Jesus isn't just about following Him on Sundays and doing our own thing the other six days. It's about living our normal everyday life following His lead. It's consistently applying His Word to our lives and doing what He did. When asked what the greatest commandment was, Jesus replied:

> *Thou shalt love the Lord thy God with all thy heart, and with all thy soul,*
> *and with all thy mind. This is the first and great commandment. And the*
> *second is like unto it, Thou shalt love thy neighbor as thyself.*
> Matthew 22:37- 39

These can't be fulfilled by doing them only part of the time. They are to be woven into the fabric of our lives. They are to be our normal whether we're on vacation or back into the routine of a Monday morning on the front porch.

(Original post July 2023)

113

July
~ 26 ~

*R*ain! It's been a long time since we were blessed with a good rain. I can't imagine what it was like in Elijah's day when it didn't rain for *three years*. Israel was under the rule of Ahab, a very wicked king. The nation turned away from God and was worshipping Baal, which included burning their own children as part of their worship. But God had a plan to turn it around. He sent His prophet Elijah with a message to the king:

And Elijah the Tishbite, who was of the inhabitants of Gilead, said unto Ahab,
As the LORD God of Israel liveth, before whom I stand, there shall not
be dew nor rain these years, but according to my word.
1 Kings 17:1

Once the drought set in, Ahab didn't seek God. He sought to kill Elijah. Interestingly, he wanted to kill the one person who had the power to break the drought. But eventually, this led to a showdown on Mt. Carmel where our God answered by fire, and the nation began to turn back to the Lord. God still knows how to turn nations.

If my people, which are called by my name, shall humble themselves, and pray,
and seek my face, and turn from their wicked ways; then will I hear
from heaven, and will forgive their sin, and will heal their land.
2 Chronicles 7:14

It's His promise. It's His Word. Let's do our part as His people.

Our land needs healing.

(Original post July 2022)

July
~ 27 ~

The fields have had their share of graceful, long-legged invaders. They happily eat the fruit of the ground that farmers work so hard to produce. Yet, I never grow tired of watching them easily bouncing through a field, white tales in the air. God made them beautiful indeed.

I've also had invaders in my life. They are time stealers, gratefully eating minutes away as I mindlessly scroll through unimportant information. It's so much better when I engage in God's Word instead. It takes a bit more mental energy as I have to pay more attention than when scrolling, but it is so worth it. God's Word encourages, directs, and comforts. Social media does..... not much.

It's okay for me to spend some time checking on friends, but if I get lost in the minutiae, I can get discouraged. I'm better off turning it off, opening the Bible app or my Bible with real pages, and then find blessing, direction, and comfort.

(Original post July 2023)

July

~ 28 ~

The sun is rising on this beautiful Sunday morning. It's going to be a great day to celebrate the risen Lord.

My body made a strong argument for staying in bed, but it lost, overruled by my mind. As a three-part being (mind, spirit, and body), although it often speaks loudly, the body doesn't get to decide my course of action. My body pulls toward ease while my spirit contends in the opposite direction. But it is my mind that makes the decision.

On the night of His betrayal, Jesus directed His disciples to pray, but they fell asleep. After a bit, He woke them with these words:

> *Watch and pray, that ye enter not into temptation: the spirit*
> *indeed is willing, but the flesh is weak.*
> Matthew 26:41

He knew they needed to be fortified with prayer to build themselves up to face what was coming. Instead, they fell asleep, and the voice of flesh won out when evil came. The spirit was willing, but their minds sided with the overwhelming voice of the flesh. It could have been different had they obeyed and been built up in prayer.

I love how one day a week is set aside to gather for praise, prayer, and hearing the Word. I need to fortify my mind so the voice crying to stay in bed is put in its proper place—subservient to the Holy Spirit. Renewing the mind means more future victories over the flesh. It's time to get ready. See you there.

(Original post July 2023)

119

July
~ 29 ~

$\mathcal{M}$y family and I spent a few days on the shores of Lake Huron and visited this lighthouse. Its light has shone brightly over the years to guide ships to safety. Light does that. It guides us safely along our way if we choose to walk in it. If we choose to walk in darkness, we are blind to hazards. Our toes suffer unnecessary stubbings at night when we walk past light switches.

Lives suffer without a Savior when we walk past the light of the world. Speaking to the people, Jesus said:

*I am light to the world, and those who embrace me will experience
life-giving light, and they will never walk in darkness.*
John 8:12 TPT

Light not only reveals danger, it also reveals who we are and gives direction. It reminds me of a hymn we used to sing in church. Its chorus still rings true:
"Oh how beautiful to walk in the steps of the Savior. Stepping in the light, stepping in the light. How beautiful to walk in the steps of the Savior, led in paths of light."
(E.E. Hewitt, 1890)

(Original post July 2022)

July
~ 30 ~

*A*fter my Bible study friends left last night, I ventured outside. It was just dark enough that the solar lights had begun to glow. They added a peaceful feeling to close a wonderful evening. We'd had a lively discussion of scripture and how to apply it to our everyday lives and relationships. I was reminded of something Joyce Meyer shared years ago about how she got along with everyone until her husband or kids woke up. It's the truth. It's easy to be at peace with everyone until we are really doing life together.

> *It takes a grinding wheel to sharpen a blade, and so one person*
> *sharpens the character of another.*
> *Proverbs 27:17 TPT*

I remember watching my dad sharpen our hoes in preparation for long days of hoeing weeds out of our bean fields. When the hoe hit the grinding wheel, sparks flew.

Sparks fly in relationships too sometimes. At times, we need to bump up against each other to sharpen and shape each other's character into the best we can be. I'm not referring to arguing or angry words, but to sharpening through open sharing of opinions.

Last night, others' thoughts stretched my thoughts on the scriptures discussed. I learned, I grew, and my "hoe" was sharpened to better accomplish the task of hoeing out weeds in the relationship fields of my tomorrows. Dad sharpened our hoes often because they grew dull and less effective with use.

I appreciate those I often meet with to discuss God's Word.

I need my hoe sharpened.

(Original post July 2023)

July
~ 31 ~

$\mathcal{T}$he sunrise had spectacular moments this morning that quickly changed. The brevity reminded me of a line from an old poem by C.T. Studd I've heard quoted in sermons: *"Only one life twill soon be past, only what's done for Christ will last."*

Our days, weeks, and even years pass quickly. I've been asked if I think these are the last days. The answer is, I don't know. Many things line up with Biblical prophecy, so they could be.

I do know we're all heading for our last days. If the world continues for another century or so, I won't. Many of us have fewer days ahead of us than behind us, so we're in our last days. Let's make them spectacular, living for Jesus.

(Original post July 2022)

As we study, we learn more of His truth,
clearing peek holes in the proverbial dark glass
so we can live better in His ways.
As we seek, our view becomes clearer and clearer.
~ Jeanne Chaffin

August
2024

August

~ 1 ~

$\mathcal{M}$y brother-in-law loves to dabble in his greenhouse, which contains a variety of beautiful blooms. These pansies have to be my favorite. I can't help but smile when I see these bright, cheerful flowers. Somehow, their dainty blooms look happy and take me back to simpler, more carefree childhood times.

Sometimes, we make life complex, dwelling on the complicated when the Lord makes it simple. Trust Him. Obey. Pray. Rejoice always. Share His love.

Jesus sent His followers out saying:

And as ye go, preach, saying, The kingdom of heaven is at hand. Heal the sick, cleanse the lepers, raise the dead, cast out devils: freely ye have received, freely give.
Matthew 10:7-8

In common vernacular, it would boil down to sharing the good news and doing the work of the ministry. The Passion Translation concluded the thought this way:

Freely you have received the power of the kingdom, so freely release it to others.

We're not to overthink the instructions we receive from the Lord and thus talk ourselves out of doing them. We're to simply obey and demonstrate God's goodness to those around us daily.

There's beauty in simplicity. There's joy in the journey.

(Original post August 2023)

August
~ 2 ~

A new day dawns with a beautiful sunrise. This morning I will go see my physical therapist to get my big toe worked on. Her gentle but firm hands help realign it every couple of weeks. The process can hurt a bit, but the results are well worth it. Afterward, I am good to walk freely again. It's amazing to me when one small part of my body is out of kilter it affects everything: first, the rest of my foot, then my knee, followed by my hip and back.

If left on my own, my thoughts and opinions seem right to me. God's Word and fellow believers often adjust my thinking, putting me back into alignment with His truth. When I go astray in one area, it impacts other parts of my life and faith walk.

Every way of a man is right in his own eyes: But the LORD pondereth the hearts.
Proverbs 21:2

He knows our motives; if we ask Him, He reveals them to us. So, again, I pray David's prayer:

Search me, O God, and know my heart: Try me, and know my thoughts: And see if there be any wicked way in me, And lead me in the way everlasting.
Psalm 139:23-24

It's time for my daily adjustment so I can walk freely again.

(Original post August 2023)

August

~ 3 ~

*T*his is my favorite table during warm months. I eat most of my meals here while listening to the sounds of nature. It's peaceful even though the chairs aren't the most comfortable, and I often have to retreat into the house to retrieve a forgotten item or two.

The table was a birthday present from years past. Unbeknownst to me, Mark had already bought me a gift when I saw this table and chair set at the local hardware and hinted rather loudly that it would make a perfect birthday gift. So that year I got two gifts. Mark was as generous as he was kind. We enjoyed this table together for years. Now I enjoy it alone. I truly do.

In the second beatitude in Matthew 5:4, the Lord promises to comfort those who mourn, and He is faithful: *"Blessed are they that mourn: for they shall be comforted."*

Comfort doesn't mean you don't miss loved ones gone on before. It also doesn't mean life returns to the same as before their passing. In this verse, the English translation for *'comforted'* is *'comfort.'* In the Greek, it is *'to be called or invited near.'* In our times of deep sorrow, the Lord calls us to come near. As we lean into the riches of His love, we draw strength for the next breath, the next moment, and the next day. When we answer the invitation to come near we are no longer alone at a table for two. We have an unseen guest joining us.

The lyrics from the chorus of the old hymn *In the Garden* by C. Austin Mills come to mind: *"And the joy we share as we tarry there, none other has ever known."* Yes, there's still joy.

Thou wilt shew me the path of life: In thy presence is fulness of joy;
At thy right hand there are pleasures for evermore.
Psalm 16:11

There is joy in the journey as I accept His invitation to come near again today and all my tomorrows. God is good.

(Original post August 2023)

August
~ 4 ~

It's early morning, and the sky is already filled with luscious colors. It's going to be a glorious sunrise. He who paints the sky is at it again. It's time to:

Arise, shine; for thy light is come, and the glory of the LORD is risen upon thee. For, behold, the darkness shall cover the earth, and gross darkness the people: but the LORD shall arise upon thee, and his glory shall be seen upon thee. And the Gentiles shall come to thy light, and kings to the brightness of thy rising.
Isaiah 60:1-3

The glory of the Lord shall rise and be seen. This verse, written centuries before Jesus came, referred to His coming. But I believe it relates to His church as well. The glory shall be seen, and it will draw others, both common folks and rulers, to His light. It's time to arise.

As my two-year-old granddaughter says when she first opens her eyes: *"It's wakey time!"*

It's wakey time, Church. The glory is rising.

(Original post August 2022)

August

~ 5 ~

I woke up early to the sound of a much-needed rain shower. It didn't last long, but hopefully, it's a precursor of what is to come as rain is predicted throughout the day. It's been a drought year.

In a drought year, a corn plant's roots go deep, searching for moisture. Deep roots are essential. They provide water and give stability in the time of a storm. As believers, we must also develop our root system and go deep down into the truths of His Word because storms and droughts can appear out of nowhere.

And now, just as you accepted Christ Jesus as your Lord, you must continue to follow him. Let your roots grow down into him, and let your lives be built on him. Then your faith will grow strong in the truth you were taught, and you will overflow with thankfulness.
Colossians 2:6-7 NLT

Truly following Jesus isn't a quick one-and-done prayer at an altar. A prayer to receive Him is only a beginning—a sprout. It needs to put roots down into the truth of the Word and grow into a lifestyle of faith. Attending church, hearing the Word explained, being part of a Bible study group where questions can be answered, and personal time in God's Word all help grow roots.

Interestingly, verse 7 doesn't guarantee that deep roots result in an easy life. It says that the end product of deep roots is that we'll overflow with thankfulness.

(Original post August 2022)

August
~ 6 ~

I awoke to a light fog in the distance. Now I'm surrounded by it. This verse comes to my mind:

Wherefore seeing we also are compassed about with so great a cloud of witnesses,
let us lay aside every weight, and the sin which doth so easily beset us,
and let us run with patience the race that is set before us.
Hebrews 12:1

Three years ago, my life was forever changed as Mark went to heaven on August 6, 2019. His legacy joins those of others who lived for the Lord, encouraging us to run our race of life in faith. Mark loved Jesus. He rose early every day to spend time with Him in His Word and in prayer. He prayed for his family, friends, neighbors and acquaintances. He prayed over his fields and those of his neighbors. Every decision was prayed over. He also acted on what he felt the Lord told him to do. He was obedient. He was kind to all and loved us all amazingly well. What an example.

Knowing his great faith and that he would be disappointed if I lived out my life in despair, I've chosen to daily put on "the garment of praise for the spirit of heaviness" (see Isaiah 61:3).

The spirit of heaviness is crushing. The Biblical way to break through it is through praise. I certainly don't praise because Mark is no longer here. I praise because he is in heaven. I praise because the Lord is faithfully walking us through. I praise because I know heaven is real, God's Word is true, and to live is Christ, and to die is gain (see Philippians 1:21).

A benefit of praise is that praising brings joy, and *"the joy of the Lord is my strength"* (Nehemiah 8:10). Without the joy of the Lord, the heaviness of grief would have made running the race of life almost as impossible as running one footed. And after last winter's foot surgeries, I know how well that works.

So today is another day to choose to put on the garment of praise. It's a choice. Some days are easier than others. Thanks to those of you who have made it easier, who have carried me and my family in prayer when we needed you the most. What a blessing you are. I encourage you all to remember Mark today and the life he lived. Let his example encourage you, as the verse says to lay aside the weight that holds you back from running your best in the race set before you.

(Original post August 2022)

August
~ 7 ~

Yesterday's sunrise was pretty. Today's skyline is devoid of sun. Clouds rule the day. I'm thankful that we have memories of days full of sun on cloudy days. Our memories help sustain us through dark times. They also remind us that our skies won't always be cloudy.

I'm reminded of a cloud-covered day a few years ago at Detroit Metro Airport. There was no sun in sight. But moments after takeoff, our plane broke through the thick layer of clouds into brilliant sun. Changing my position changed my physical outlook.

Following long periods of wakefulness in the middle of the night, I got up feeling like a rock this morning. I wasn't discouraged, but just moving took more effort than usual. Breakthrough wasn't happening so when I got in the shower, I forced myself to sing. I didn't feel like it. I also didn't sing songs that matched my feelings. I started with the old hymn *"Sweeter as the Years Go By,"* by Mrs. C. H. Morris. By the time I finished it, the weights were dropping off, and one song turned into a praise concert. I had purposely adjusted my attitude to change my outlook.

I've learned over the years that, as Nehemiah 8:10 says, *"The joy of the Lord is my strength."* But to enter His joy, I have to do something. It doesn't just fall on me out of the sky. Isaiah 61:3 states that He has given us a garment of praise for a spirit of heaviness. In other words, if we have a spirit of heaviness and feel like we're carrying the weight of the world, He has given us a garment of praise to set us free.

Today I just needed to put the garment on by praising Him. God's Word always has the answer to our current condition. Sometimes, we have to force ourselves to make the necessary adjustments, but when we do, we reap the benefits. Changing my position took effort this morning, but now *"I've got sunshine on a cloudy day."* If you're near my age, you know the next line. But I'm not talkin' 'bout my girl, as the song says. I'm talkin' 'bout my God.

(Original post August 2023)

August

~ 8 ~

The sun looks enormous in the morning sky, but it appears small in the picture. Sometimes things in our lives seem like a big deal, but they aren't so grand in the big picture. Sometimes, we make a mountain out of a molehill, but God's Word directs us to speak to the mountain in our life and cast it into the sea (see Mark 11:23-24).

We're not to talk about the mountain in our lives. We're not to complain to the Lord about our mountain's size. We're to talk to the mountain and tell it how mighty our God is. Nowhere in the Bible are believers referred to as victims; instead, we are called victors. We're not the overcome; we're called overcomers. Mountains of circumstance aren't to rule over us. We are to reign over them by using our voices to declare God's Word over our situation.

"Oh, woe is me" keeps me in bondage. *"I can do all things through Christ which strengtheneth me"* (Philippians 4:13) sets me free. *"Death and life are in the power of the tongue"* (Proverbs 18:21a).

What we say is important. Our tongues make molehills large, but with faith in our hearts, our tongues bring mountains down.

Speak wisely. Words are powerful.

(Original post August 2023)

August
~ 9 ~

This area of my yard hasn't shown up in many pictures. It's not been an area I was so proud of. It was functional but needed to be spruced up a bit. I'd tried some things to make it better, but my efforts were fruitless. But out of the blue, a friend from high school dropped off two beautiful lilies. They look a little droopy due to being transplanted recently, but once they settle in, the vibrant peach and yellow colors will bring this area to life.

I couldn't be happier! Where my efforts fell short, the help of a friend came through. I'm so thankful. Each time I look upon this spot through my kitchen window, I'll see the lilies and be refreshed, remembering the kindness of my friend.

Sweet friendships refresh the soul and awaken our hearts with joy, for good friends are like the anointing oil that yields the fragrant incense of God's presence.
Proverbs 27:9 TPT

The fragrant incense of God's presence, indeed.

(Original post August 2023)

August

~ 10 ~

$\mathcal{O}$ne of my new lilies bloomed already, a luscious yellow with frayed edges on its pedals. It is perfectly created and magnificently displayed.

Sometimes, we worry about our frayed edges. We compare ourselves to others, believing we come up short, not realizing that our frayed edges define us and make us unique. What we see in ourselves as weakness, others view as God's grace working through us.

In answer to Paul's request to be free of frays, Paul records God's response:

But he said to me, "My grace is sufficient for you, for my power is made perfect in weakness." Therefore, I will boast all the more gladly about my weaknesses, so that Christ's power may rest on me. That is why, for Christ's sake, I delight in weaknesses, in insults, in hardships, in persecutions, in difficulties. For when I am weak, then I am strong.
2 Corinthians 12:9-10 NIV

Paul's frayed edges of weakness and persecutions were made gracefully beautiful in the Master's hand. When we surrender, ours will be too. My new lilies originated in my friend's son's garden. He is a master breeder of lilies. I'm sure the beautifully frayed edges were by design, not by accident.

When I feel inadequate or insignificant, I remind myself that my frayed edges become strength when I place them in the Master's hands. His grace is more than enough, frayed edges and all.

(Original post August 2023)

August

~ 11 ~

The sun is rising over another day on the farm, and guys have already been working. It's cool on my front porch this morning, so I'm wrapped in a blanket, and it feels good.

I love the stillness of the early morning. It's my favorite time to read, pray, and reflect. As I wrote the date this morning, I was reminded that today would have been my grandmother's birthday. Grandma lived with us for seven years and helped shape my life. She never complained and never gave unsolicited advice. She was a very wise woman and a great example. She had many years of life experiences when she came to live with us.

Experience is a good teacher, and it's easy to want to share what we've learned with others. But if it isn't welcomed, or is repeated often, it becomes annoying; as Proverbs says: *"A continual dropping in a very rainy day..."* (see Proverbs 27:15).

So Lord:

Set a guard over my mouth, Lord; keep watch over the door of my lips.
Psalms 141:3 NIV

Let me be like my grandma, who loved unconditionally and shared her wisdom upon request. Grandma's words were golden, not only because they were wise but also because she waited to share them at the right time.

Winsome words spoken at just the right time are as appealing as apples
gilded in gold surrounded with silver.
Proverbs 25:11 TPT

(Original post August 2023)

August

~ 12 ~

*T*he moon shone brightly over the farm last night as we get closer to a full moon. I enjoy moonlight as it illuminates the night sky.

Years ago, as I was preparing to go on a mission trip to the Dominican Republic with the campus ministry that my son leads, it occurred to me that I would be south of Cuba in July. I don't do heat well and I panicked that it would be too much heat for me. I remember sitting on my front porch wondering why I let him talk me into going and praying it would somehow work out. I had my Bible on my lap, opened it randomly, and began to read these words:

The sun shall not smite thee by day, Nor the moon by night.
Psalm 121:6

I remember exclaiming to the Lord: *"I'm not worried about moon smite, but thanks for sun smite protection."* I don't recommend the open-and-point method, but it was right on that day. My worry ended. The whole time we were in the Dominican Republic, while students worked with the sweet orphan children in the hot sun, I was always assigned a shaded area to work with them. It was sweltering there, but I was protected from sun smite. And the moon over the island didn't smite me either.

He is faithful.

(Original post August 2022)

August

~ 13 ~

And the night shall become light around me.
Psalms 139:11

The heavy cloud cover in most of the sky makes the horizon area devoid of clouds appear extremely bright and beautiful. Night is surrendering to light seemingly in inches today. There is a definite division of where light starts and darkness ends.

In the book of John, it states that Jesus is the Light of the world. In the most quoted Bible scripture, it says:

For God so loved the world, that he gave his only begotten Son, that whosoever believeth in him should not perish, but have everlasting life.
John 3:16

A few verses later, it's followed with:

And this is the condemnation, that light is come into the world, and men loved darkness rather than light, because their deeds were evil.
John 3:19

Darkness surrendered in inches, but light won. The cross beat darkness at its own game, paying the price to ransom the lost. It made a way in the darkness for whosoever will come. The invitation is still open.

If you openly declare that Jesus is Lord and believe in your heart that God raised him from the dead, you will be saved. For it is by believing in your heart that you are made right with God, and it is by openly declaring your faith that you are saved.
Romans 10:9-10

(Original post August 2022)

August
~ 14 ~

$\mathcal{Y}$esterday's sunrise photographed as fire in the sky. The colors were much softer with more dark blue, but you wouldn't know it from the photo. Sometimes, things and people show up differently than they truly are.

Jesus warned his followers to watch out for *"wolfs dressed in sheep's clothing"* (see Matthew 7:15). It was a visual warning about those who intentionally mislead and deceive. The deceivers cause "the sheep"—metaphorically speaking of believers—to question their faith and destroy them. Real wolves don't just toy with sheep; they eat them for lunch.

Their tactics are as old as those used in the Garden of Eden as they hissed the question: *"Did God really say....?"* Their strategy is to attack God's Word. It's important that we know what God's Word says so we're not easy prey.

When Jesus heard the hissed questions as He was tempted, He didn't respond with what He thought, what He heard someone else say, or how He felt. He responded with scripture. If *He* needed to respond using God's Word, I do too.

It's not time to stop going to church or stop studying to learn more of God's Word. It's the only ammunition that works against wolves.

(Original post August 2022)

August
~ 15 ~

Sunrise reminded me of the glittering effect in the sky following fireworks. The clouds filtered the light, giving it an unusually intriguing look.

Clouds impact our lives. Hard times can attempt to blot out the influence of God's Word in our lives. But when we continue to apply the Word of God in our lives, His love and peace shine through our clouds. It may look unusual, but that will draw others to it because they will see it's real. Anyone can rejoice in the Lord in good times, but to see someone rejoicing in the midst of troubles is beautifully intriguing.

James tells us our response to trouble is to rejoice:

Consider it pure joy, my brothers and sisters, whenever you face trials of many kinds.
James 1:2 NIV

The norm is to consider it a pain, a nuisance, or a worry—anything but joy. How we consider it drives our response. We become angry, annoyed, or anxious if we consider it according to the previous list of normal feelings. Considering it pure joy reveals our deep trust in our Father God.

If we continue reading the next couple of verses, we will find out that as we rely on Him in good times and bad, we develop perseverance, which matures our faith. Our reason for joy isn't the trouble itself. It's the final impact it has in our lives. We know that our God will turn our test into a testimony. Our joyful response allows the Light of the world to glitter in the clouds of our lives, intriguing those around us and bringing hope to those facing similar trials.

Our decision on how we consider our circumstances determines whether our skies glitter or are gloomy. Consistently choosing joy is key.

(Original post August 2023)

August
~ 16 ~

The sky is warming up with a rosy pink, and the air is cool. It's going to be a beautiful day. It will also be a busy one. I have peaches to can and corn to freeze. It's that time on the farm; time to preserve the goodness of summer so it can be savored throughout the winter. The preservation takes time and energy, but it's worth the effort.

If we buy into the *"live for today"* culture, we miss out on much. Tomorrow will come, so we need to prepare for it. Even nature gives us examples of preparing:

Go to the ant, you sluggard; consider its ways and be wise! It has no commander, no overseer or ruler, yet it stores its provisions in summer and gathers its food at harvest.
Proverbs 6:6-8 NIV

We don't just prepare with canning and freezing. We save our income so we can pay cash or have rainy days' funds for emergencies. We also prepare by storing His Word in our hearts.

Thy word have I hid in mine heart, That I might not sin against thee.
Psalm 119:10-11

Storing His Word through memorization gives us the ability to pull it off our mind's 'shelf' when we need it, just like I can pull a jar of peaches off the shelf in my cupboard when I need to bake a pie.

Sitting in my glider rocker on the porch sounds like a great idea this morning, but gliding won't accomplish the task at hand. The ants are busy, so I should be too.

(Original post August 2023)

August

~ 17 ~

A couple of days ago, the peach tree branches were bent down, heavy with fruit. As we picked, freeing the branches from the weight, they sprang back up. Bearing fruit was costly for the tree. Time, energy, and resources went into growing every delicious peach. The tree's loaded branches bore the ever-increasing weight over the growing season until harvest finally came. Yet, the fruit didn't benefit the tree. The tree won't enjoy warm peach pies or the wonderful flavor of canned peaches on a cold winter's day. The fruit was for others.

The Bible calls us to be fruit bearers. We are to produce the fruit of the Holy Spirit. The King James translation is familiar:

But the fruit of the Spirit is love, joy, peace, longsuffering, gentleness, goodness, faith, meekness, temperance: against such there is no law.
Galatians 5:22-23

But the Passion Translation speaks more clearly to me:

But the fruit produced by the Holy Spirit within you is divine love in all its varied expressions: joy that overflows, peace that subdues, patience that endures, kindness in action, a life full of virtue, faith that prevails, gentleness of heart, and strength of spirit. Never set the law above these qualities, for they are meant to be limitless.
Galatians 5:22-23 TPT

Whichever translation, the overall message is that we are to live with our "branches" laden with fruit for others to pick and benefit from. In so doing, we give others a taste of the Father's attributes, and they'll find, as the Psalmist wrote:

O taste and see that the LORD is good: Blessed is the man that trusteth in him.
Psalm 34:8

(Original post August 2023)

August
~ 18 ~

These two are quite the pair. Ten-year-old Titus is a friend to all and is especially beloved by his little cousin, Vivian. She loves him fiercely with all the love in her 4-year-old heart because, since she was small, he has taken time out of other things he could be doing to play with her. And his kindness has been rewarded with many specially created works of art and over-the-top greetings. Kindness doesn't go unnoticed.

Titus was named after the Apostle Paul's friend of the same name. Paul called him a dear son and loyal friend. Just as Paul commended 1st century Titus for his love, his steadfast faith, and for bringing comfort to others, it could truly be said of this Titus who is giving kindness and encouragement to friends, teammates, and even his little cousin.

Even a child is known by his doings, whether his work
be pure and whether it be right.
Proverbs 20:11

If children are known by their doing, so are we. So let us be known for our kindness, honesty, and incredible love as we love others as He first loved us.

(This was not originally posted in a previous August, but it fulfills a promise to a grandson that he would be in my next book.)

August
~ 19 ~

A few days ago, I spent the day processing and freezing sweet corn. It's a task I've done since childhood. My dad and brother used to pick and husk the corn. Mom organized the process and handled the blanching and cooling part. Then Dad cut the kernels off the cob. I bagged the kernels, and my brother carried the remaining corncobs out and dumped them in the field to decompose. It was a family endeavor that we carried out yearly in the cool of our basement.

Over the years, we dwindled in number until it was just mom and me in her basement. When schedules allowed, my daughters-in-love joined in, but typically it was Mom who consistently did her part through her 96th year, and I picked up the remaining pieces of the puzzle.

For the last couple of years, sometimes a grandchild, who was being trained as a bagger, joined me. But often, it's just me and a flood of memories. What made it special was that we all had a role to play. We all were important in the process, whether husker, blancher, bagger, or cob remover. We all had a purpose.

The life of the church is similar. We all have an important role to play in the process: a greeter; usher; Sunday school teacher; prayer warrior, or pastor.

For his "body" has been formed in his image and is closely joined together and constantly connected as one. And every member has been given divine gifts to contribute to the growth of all; and as these gifts operate effectively throughout the whole body, we are built up and made perfect in love.
Ephesians 4:16 TPT

Just as each part of our bodies is important, so is each part of a church body. Each of us is important in the process. We all have a purpose.

(Original post August 2023)

August
~ 20 ~

This little rascal stopped by, seemingly curious about what I was doing. He bravely got fairly close and gave me a good look before scurrying off to take refuge in a nearby tree. Places of refuge are good.

> God is our refuge and strength, A very present help in trouble. Therefore, will not we fear, though the earth be removed, And though the mountains be carried into the midst of the sea.
> Psalm 46:1-2

God is our place to scurry to. He is our help, even if mountains, or as another translation phrases it, *"our every source of support"* is carried into the sea. His shelter is still available.

Over the past few years, it's where I've run. His refuge is hidden in His word. I haven't audibly heard Him speak, yet in the difficult moments as I turn to Him for help, a scripture will rise to the surface. I take peace and strength from it, thus taking refuge in that Word of the Lord.

As with my furry-tailed visitor, we have a place to run and hide in the strong branches that safely hold us, even in the midst of trouble.

(Original post August 2022)

August
~ 21 ~

Seasons are changing. The sun is rising later. Yesterday it was still dark when I came to the porch. School sessions are starting. Soon, football games and cider will be on the horizon.

How quickly time goes by. It seems that summer just started, and now it's finishing. Life is like that. The Bible refers to it as a vapor:

Whereas ye know not what shall be on the morrow. For what is your life? It is even a vapor, that appeareth for a little time, and then vanisheth away.
James 4:14

The point is that it goes quickly. The passage goes on to tell us not to get so caught up in things we plan to do in the future that we miss opportunities to be a blessing today. A few verses later, the chapter concludes with:

So if you know of an opportunity to do the right thing today, yet you refrain from doing it, you're guilty of sin.
James 4:17 TPT

It's so easy to miss daily opportunities. Life is busy. I often think that later I will get to what I feel the Lord is nudging me toward, but when I put off doing it, I frequently forget. The opportunity is lost. I call it busyness. God calls it sin.

Yikes. It's time for a change. Ideas that float to the surface aren't to stew on the back burner but are God-ideas to be acted upon.

So teach us to number our days, That we may apply our hearts unto wisdom.
Psalm 90:12

(Original post August 2023)

August

~ 22 ~

*M*y brother just finished painting his barn. This is the back of it, and I should have taken pictures of the front as well. It's an old barn that now looks great. It used to be my grandparents' barn, but it even predates their ownership. It was built to last, but without necessary maintenance over the years, it wouldn't have.

Relationships are similar. Many are built well, but over the years little issues have come up that, if unresolved, lead to larger ones and take their toll.

Do not let the sun go down while you are still angry,
Ephesians 4:26b NIV

In other words, don't go to bed mad. Stay up a little late if you need to, and work it out. Letting it fester will make it bigger. Resolving problems when they're small helps keep relationships and barns strong.

(Original post August 2022)

August

~ 23 ~

Summer flower bouquets are the best. This one was a gift from my daughter-in-love that came from her friend's roadside booth. It's beautiful and makes me smile whenever it catches my eye. Knowing flowers were freshly gathered with me in mind and artistically arranged feels like a warm hug.

I've heard people compare God to a gardener making a bouquet. At times of great loss and grief, for lack of things to say, they try to comfort by saying things inferring that the loved one was chosen because God needed another flower in His bouquet. I know of some who were very hurt thinking of God as a very mean gardener for taking their loved one away for such a frivolous reason. Of course, the flower-gathering idea isn't Biblical.

I believe scripture shows that believers who die are welcomed home, hopefully with a *"...Well done, good and faithful servant..."* (see Matthew 25:23). The Lord receives us. He doesn't reach down and pluck us up for a flower gathering in the sky. We serve a good and loving God, the author of life (see Acts 3:15 NLT). He is the one who comforts the brokenhearted (see Matthew 5:4).

God's comforted me more than once. He will comfort you as well. The flower bouquets are for us who are alive and remain. When the time comes, we will be welcomed into His loving arms in our new home, which will need no earthly flowers.

(Original post August 2023)

August
~ 24 ~

A crescent moon greeted me this early morning, as did the planet Venus. In this picture, Venus is below and to the left of the moon, a little above the horizon. At least Google says it's Venus. My knowledge of planets is mainly limited to the one called Earth.

It is helpful to be able to go online to find answers to questions like, *"What planet is visible currently?"* Google answers quickly. But there are answers even Google doesn't know. Questions like how to go on after a devastating loss, how to have joy amid sadness, and how to experience an abundant life are not so easily answered. Only Jesus can answer questions of the heart. Only He can fill the void. Only He came to give abundant life (see John 10:10). He said the Holy Spirit would lead us into all truth (see John 16:13). I take Him at His word.

Some heart answers have come quickly. Some have taken their time. Others I still seek, but I'm promised if I seek, I'll find. If I knock, the door will be opened (see Matthew 7:7). Sometimes I need to grow in faith to receive my answer. Just as we can't always give a full answer to a 2-year-old's question, the Lord can't always fully answer ours. It's not that He doesn't know the answer, but at the present we can't comprehend it. As we grow and develop, we're ready for more detail.

So as the children's song says, *"I'll read my Bible pray every day and I'll grow, grow, grow"* (by Harry D. Clarke). Answers will come, and in the meantime, I will trust and keep walking by faith.

He is faithful.

(Original post August 2022)

August

~ 25 ~

I caught a glimpse of the fluttering wings of a black swallowtail butterfly and quickly went to get a closer look. From a distance, I saw a beautiful fluttering butterfly. When I got closer, I saw a butterfly that was a little worse for wear, missing part of its lower right wing.

Most of us are like this butterfly. From a distance we look ok, but up close, we are a little worse for wear. We are scared and carry wounds of past seasons. Thankfully, when given to the Lord, scars heal, and the tests we've gone through can turn into testimonies that can be used to help others.

Only the Lord can make beauty out of our ashes and give us the oil of joy for mourning (see Isaiah 61:3). He doesn't just get us through; he redeems, restores, beautifies, and gives us joy in the journey. The key is giving our wounds to Him. Trusting Him with them begins the restorative process.

Ashes are melting into beauty. Testimonies of hope are coming. Joy is rebirthed in our hearts. Trust in the One who alone is able. He never fails.

(Original post August 2023)

August
~ 26 ~

I awoke to this beautiful sky as a crest of sunlight was just awakening in the northeastern sky. It gave anticipation for a good day ahead. Light does that. It shines and sparkles, adding interest to our world.

Last night, light shined in fireflies. My littles were spending the night, and after a busy day playing outside, we stayed up to give chase. The glowing bugs weren't as prevalent as earlier in the summer, but there were enough for them to make laughter fill the air with shouts of *"There's one."* The bugs proved to be elusive, and only a few were scooped up in little hands, causing some tears of disappointment to flow.

Thankfully, the Light of the world isn't difficult to catch. We don't have to run hither and thither or ascend to the top of a mountain to find His truth. God is near us, waiting to be found.

> But we receive the faith-righteousness that speaks an entirely different message: "Don't for a moment think you need to climb into the heavens to find the Messiah and bring him down, or to descend into the underworld to bring him up from the dead." But the faith-righteousness we receive speaks to us in these words of Moses: "God's living message is very close to you, as close as your own heart beating in your chest and as near as the tongue in your mouth." And what is God's "living message"? It is the revelation of faith for salvation, which is the message that we preach. For if you publicly declare with your mouth that Jesus is Lord and believe in your heart that God raised him from the dead, you will experience salvation. The heart that believes in him receives the gift of the righteousness of God—and then the mouth confesses, resulting in salvation. For the Scriptures encourage us with these words: "Everyone who believes in him will never be disappointed.
> Romans 10:6-11 TPT

If you haven't already received the Light of the world, just ask and receive. Catch the light. It's the catch of a lifetime.

(Original post August 2023)

August
~ 27 ~

I woke up to gray skies and had little hope of taking a pretty picture today. But suddenly, the sky changed from black and white to soft pastels. It was like a developing photograph. In the first part of the process, we can't see how it will turn out, but God does. He declares the end from the beginning (see Isaiah 46:10). He knows the plans He has for us, and He says those plans are good to give us a hope and a future (see Jeremiah 29:11).

If we feel like our days are dark with little hope, perhaps we are in the darkroom going through the development process. In the days of film photography, I remember having my camera open accidentally exposing the film prematurely. The early exposure ruined whatever image the film had captured. Similarly, sometimes, we're not ready to walk into our plan yet. We can't even see it on the horizon, but He can and knows how to develop the image He placed within us.

Delight thyself also in the LORD; And he shall give thee the desires of thine heart.
Psalm 37:4

He places the desires in our hearts, and then He works with us to bring them about. Our part is delighting in Him. The Hebrew word for delight could have also been translated to be soft or pliable. We're to be pliable in His gentle hands as He develops the desires in our hearts.

Take heart. He's not finished with us yet. The picture is still developing.

(Original post August 2022)

August
~ 28 ~

It looks like another beautiful day. Mine started with an early morning fasting blood draw. I was at the hospital at the beginning of the day so I could come home to breakfast. Breakfast has always been a favorite meal, even if it's only a bowl of cereal. My body wakes up ready to eat. It's funny about our bodies; we may have eaten three squares plus snacks yesterday, but today's a new day and yesterday's meals are long gone.

Yesterday was Sunday, and I enjoyed a full course "meal" of God's Word, nicely cut up into manageable bites. It was easily digested so I could apply it to my life. But that was yesterday. Just as I don't eat only one physical meal per week, I don't thrive on just one spiritual meal weekly. I need my daily bread. So, prior to leaving my house, I spent time doing an online devotion that other women from church do also. Then, on my drive, I listened to a brief teaching on prayer. Spiritual food nourished my soul.

Hopefully, I'll either listen or read another morsel later in the day. My spirit will be ready for another treat.

(Original post August 2023)

August
~ 29 ~

The sun was setting as I drove by the bins last night. From this view, they loom larger than from my front porch sunrise side. It saddens me that Mark didn't get to see them completed. He helped Ben dream them, and saw them in his mind's eye, but before construction began, he was gone. What a gift it is to be able to visualize something before it is reality.

Faith is the substance of things hoped for, the evidence of things unseen.
Hebrews 11:1

The bins weren't all Mark saw through eyes of faith. He saw people coming to God that others may have given up on, and he prayed regularly for them.

The bins started as only a dream. The dream took on substance first in faith, and then it came forth in concrete and metal. If we wait to believe it until we can see it, we won't see it. It's true with physical buildings, and it's true in the spirit.

It's not difficult; we frequently work through the process in the negative. We worry about something that could happen. Our worry and anxieties become the substance of things feared for and the evidence of things unseen. They grow in our minds until they become our realities and limitations.

Give all your worries and cares to God, for he cares s about you.
1 Peter 5:7 NLT

We need to stop worry in its stracks. Then, get to work and replace anxious thoughts with what God's Word has to say on the subject. The more we think about or meditate on God's answer, the more faith for His answer builds in our hearts. This faith builds into substance, and over time, faith-substance turns into reality. Don't give up. Don't quit, and don't give in to stewing on doubts and "what ifs" of the enemy that undermine your faith.

Faith triumphs over fear, just like light over darkness and good over evil.

(Original post August 2023)

185

August

~ 30 ~

My swing set is missing something. It's hard to see it in this photo, but after years of use, the two-person glider broke. The littles want me to replace it with a new one just like the old one. The problem is they don't seem to make them like that anymore. So we're coming up with a new plan. The new plan wasn't readily accepted. It wasn't easy giving up on the idea of flying high in the glider or no longer being able to use it as part of a swing set obstacle course. Letting go of the past and moving forward can be difficult. Yet life will go on. The glider will be replaced with a new accessory, which is yet to be determined.

Often, when the Lord has new things for us, we want to cling to the old. We long to fly again with Him on our gliders when He has new experiences and plans for us instead.

Remember ye not the former things, neither consider the things of old. Behold, I will do a new thing; now it shall spring forth; shall ye not know it? I will even make a way in the wilderness, and rivers in the desert.
Isaiah 43:18-19

Some my age remember and long for the days of the Jesus movement. It was an amazing move of God, but God is doing a new thing. The new move won't be the same. It won't be new wine in old wine skins (see Luke 5:37-39).

We don't want to hold on to our old gliders and miss soaring on the wings of the next move of God. Get ready Church. Awakening is coming. It won't look like the past. It will be more powerful. It will make a way in our current wilderness and bring rivers to our dry lands, reaching those we may see as unreachable with the good news kingdom of God.

Get ready to soar.

(Original post August 2023)

August

~ 31 ~

Today, we close the book on August. I've taken several photos already this morning, and the sun's not even up yet. The sky is putting on a show. From the looks of things, our last day in August will be beautiful.

I write goals at the beginning of each month: people I hope to spend time with, books I want to read, and projects I want to accomplish. Tonight, I'll get out my journal to see how I've done and to set goals for September. It keeps me moving ahead. My journal also has daily sections, which really help me stay on track if I use them.

A section to list what I'm thankful for is at the beginning of each day, and at the day's end there's a place to reflect on daily highlights. I'm happier and more focused when I take the time to fill it out. A familiar verse in Psalms states:

So teach us to number our days, That we may apply our hearts unto wisdom.
Psalm 90:12

I love the King James Version, but I found the wording of that verse in The Message Bible interesting:

Oh! Teach us to live well! Teach us to live wisely and well!

I'm thankful my sweet daughter-in-love introduced me to this kind of journal at just the right time. It helps me live well. What a blessing.

I've already taken my 12th picture of the sky's splendor. It just keeps getting better and better. It's going to be a good day.

(Original post August 2022)

Epilogue

*W*hen I pulled into my driveway last night following my book signing, I noticed these well-loved toy tractors that my youngest farmers had left out. This hidden yard area is theirs to dig up and farm, be it rain or shine or in the mud from their last farming endeavor. The tractors are showing wear and tear as a second generation of farmers is now using them.

Their dads used them to farm many fields of play in days gone by. It was a melancholy moment as the site warmed my heart and reminded me who I am: a farm girl, a mom, and a grandma who loves Jesus, family, and friends.

The writing adventure the Lord has had me on for the last three-plus years is the surprise of a lifetime. If the Lord can use me to write a book, He can use anyone to accomplish any dream He drops into their hearts.

I used to think Psalm 37:4, *"Delight thyself also in the LORD; And he shall give thee the desires of thine heart,"* meant that if I delighted in the Lord, He would give me what I wanted. Now, I see that my delighting in the Lord provided an opening for Him to place a desire in my heart, something that was out of reach for me, and then He brought it to pass.

That's what He did for me. That's what He will do for you. To God be the glory! His ways are higher than our ways and His thoughts are higher than our thoughts (see Isaiah 55:7).

Who would have ever thought it was possible - only God.

(Original post August 2023)

Made in the USA
Columbia, SC
20 October 2024